Julie Enfield

Kiss and Tell

An Intimate History of Kissing

HarperCollins*PublishersLtd*

Kiss and Tell
© 2004 by Julie Enfield. All rights reserved.

Published by HarperCollins Publishers Ltd

No part of this book may be used or reproduced in any manner whatsoever without the prior written permission of the publisher, except in the case of brief quotations embodied in reviews.

First Edition

HarperCollins books may be purchased for educational, business, or sales promotional use through our Special Markets Department.

HarperCollins Publishers Ltd
2 Bloor Street East, 20th Floor
Toronto, Ontario, Canada
M4W 1A8

www.harpercanada.com

National Library of Canada Cataloguing in Publication

Enfield, Julie
Kiss and tell : an intimate history of kissing / Julie Enfield. – 1st ed.

ISBN 0-00-200634-0

1. Kissing – History. 2. Kissing – Social aspects. I. Title.

GT2640.E54 2004   394   C2003-905637-6

DWF 9 8 7 6 5 4 3 2 1

Printed and bound in Canada
Set in Trump Mediaeval

For my mother

Contents

An Encounter ix

Part One: A Sensory Oasis

1. What's in a Kiss? 3
2. Alchemy of a Kiss 10
3. A Panoply of Kisses: The Origins of Desire 21
4. Kissing and the Five Senses 66
5. Chemistry of Love 107

Part Two: A Landscape of Kisses

6. The Art of Kissing 127
7. Kissing by the Book 152

8 Cinematic Kisses   170
9 Lipstick: Elixir of Seduction   192

Epilogue: Encounter Redux   210
Acknowledgements   212
Bibliography   214
Index   222

An Encounter

He was late. It was a sweltering August afternoon in Venice, in 1997. I was standing in St. Mark's Square beside its lofty, winged lion statue waiting for the most brilliant, handsome man I had ever met, when suddenly it started to pour. He appeared, black umbrella in hand, as my mascara streamed into two dark lagoons on my cheeks, and whatever body my hair had mustered through the heat was washed out by the Venetian rain. He didn't speak. He took me in his arms—as the umbrella clattered to the cobbles—and gave me the dreamiest kiss I'd ever known. Instantly, deliriously, I knew that he was mine.

It was the memory of this potent kiss and others like it that first inspired me to begin this book. My lifelong interest in human behaviour, art and history propelled me to explore this most powerful and evocative gesture from various perspectives: cultural, chemical, physiological, literary, psychological, visual, and even technological. I would find out about the erotic—the intricacies and mysteries of kissing that transport us.

Everything begins with a kiss. We are born in our parents' first kiss and our earliest memories are of our mothers' fond kisses. Of the kisses that follow, none seems more intense than our first romantic kiss. Throughout our lives, we are kissed by fortune, by love. We learn to shape our most passionate desires with our lips.

Like anyone else, my first knowledge of kissing was born of experience. But to write this book I drew on my journalistic background and approached the topic as an investigator might. I discovered that most cultures greet one another face to face, including mouth-to-mouth kissing, cheek kissing, nose kissing, or sniff-salutations. I was surprised to find that some cultures don't kiss at all—they find kissing on the lips distasteful. Still others kiss voraciously, sucking and biting each other's lips until they bleed. And kissing is not exclusive to humans. Bonobo apes—the only primates apart from humans to copulate face to face—also kiss, probing deeply with their tongues. Anthropologists say that lips remind us of the labia, due to the fact that they billow out and flush crimson when excited, and that women may lick their lips as an unconscious way of reminding men of their other mouth. Thus the popularity of brightly hued lipsticks.

AN ENCOUNTER

I learned that when we kiss, a torrent of smell and taste sensations whirl through our system. Each kiss stirs our olfactory sites and carries the potential to activate powerful, pleasurable feelings. And a rhapsody of odours can elicit thrilling limbic memories, from that part of the brain that governs arousal. The seduction of one sense seduces another.

"What is the brain trying to tell the body?" I regularly asked. When we kiss and the sparks fly, we are said to have the right "chemistry." Great kissing produces an adrenaline-like neurochemical explosion, and the desire to kiss seems to be predicated on the readiness to procreate. But a scientific interpretation of kissing has almost always proven too cold and sterile for us. Instead, many cultures around the world have elevated and immortalized the kiss to the status of icon.

I discovered lovers, real and fictional, whose kisses could still set pulses racing hundreds of years after they were first recorded. I mapped the journey of kissing through art: portrayed on murals or canvases; carved in stone, wood or bronze; captured on paper. I gazed at screen stars fusing carnal caresses with provocative imagery, their kisses mute yet intensely eloquent.

A discourse on kissing history, habits and love can be a passageway into the more familiar zone of how we kiss as lovers. What I explore in this book is the ancestry and alchemy of kissing, how kisses vary from culture to culture, their spiritual dimensions, their erotic depths, their artistic allure, their language, their magic. *Kiss and Tell: An Intimate History of Kissing* seeks to unveil the secrets and ancient origins of this ubiquitous activity. We shall discover how kissing can transport us into an oasis of sensory delights—how vision, touch, taste, smell and sound all intermingle with our kisses. It is my hope that this book will serve as a guide to the mysteries of kissing and that it will encourage the sensualist to search deeper in her or his soul for the ultimate kiss encounter.

Part 1
A Sensory Oasis

Chapter 1
What's in a Kiss?

What is a kiss? Why this, as some approve:
The sure, sweet cement, glue, and lime of love.
—"A Kiss," Robert Herrick (1591–1674)

We kiss when we meet, when we part, when we adore. Kisses express respect, compassion and affection. We kiss our children's drowsy eyelids good-night and their scrapes to "make it better." A kiss can be a pious act; we kiss idols, altars and temples in moments of divine adoration. A kiss can be a prelude, a pledge, a provocation. We kiss to seal a promise, as in marriage, but we also kiss to deceive. We kiss to seduce. We SWAK a letter (seal with a kiss), and we smooch our pooches.

In every kiss is the promise of a thousand more. We kiss through seasons, across generations and over continents; we press our lips to photographs, locks of hair—any wistful memento of a beloved. With a pucker and blow we send our farewell kisses rushing through the air like a volley of Cupid's arrows. We feel delight each time our lips touch the same spot on a glass that our lover's lips have caressed. We leave lip graffiti on steamy mirrors. Not just sentimentalists, we kiss out of superstition: we kiss dice before we roll them, kiss amulets for good fortune, kiss under the mistletoe; we kiss the very ground beneath our feet.

There are chaste kisses and there are hungry kisses. There are wild, unbridled kisses. There are kisses whispery and soft as falling snow, kisses that cascade over everything, thrilling, rapturous. When we kiss, all the senses are involved in a vortex of passion. Kissing, we drink the sweet spirits of each other's mouths.

A kiss is born in a place and at a time of passion. A deep kiss implies more than a perfunctory movement of the lips, it implies a sentient response (from the Latin *sentire*, to feel). Kisses given without feeling are merely ritual smacks. What a kiss needs to be compelling is the ability to transcend the limit of our body. The secret is hidden in the Latin word *transcendere*—to climb or to exceed. Such transcendence registers on the lips, too, and when we kiss amorously, electrical impulses leap from our lips. At its most pure, a kiss is a symbolic fusion, a physical allegory that leads its participants to combine souls—to become one. This exquisite

What is a kiss if not the language of the heart? In love's vocabulary we buss, caress, kiss, lock lips, lollygag, make out, neck, nip, nuzzle, osculate, peck, sip, smack, smooch, sniff, spoon, taste, tease and tongue-tickle.

alchemy is best described in the nineteenth-century poet Alfred, Lord Tennyson's "Locksley Hall": "And our spirits rush'd together / at the touching of the lips."

Prelude to a Kiss

> *With a kiss let us set out*
> *for an unknown world.*
> —"La Nuit de mai," Alfred de Musset (1810–1857)

How did kissing begin? Some anthropologists theorize that the mouth kiss is a by-product of "pre-mastication," a primeval practice that involved the transfer of soft, pre-masticated food (usually chewed by the mother) into the mouth of an infant. (Many animals continue to feed their young mouth-to-mouth: chimpanzees "kiss-feed" pre-masticated bananas to their babies and lionesses regurgitate food from a kill into the mouths of their cubs.) Others contend that the kiss has its roots in tactile pleasure—we all delight in the soft caress of a partner's lips. This passion for touch may have evolved from the earliest sexual union of unicellular organisms, which, in order to exchange their hereditary nuclei, fuse in a fertilizing, albeit fleeting, "kiss."

Perhaps it shouldn't come as a surprise that kissing seems as natural to us as breathing. Kissing is an instinct. To comprehend what this means we have to go back to before we

> Scientific studies show that most of us prefer to turn our heads to the right when kissing. This right-turning preference is thought to be imprinted in the womb, where embryos favour turning their heads to the right in the last trimester before birth. This same right-turning bias could explain why many people also favour the use of the right hand.

were born. The mouth is the first facial feature to form in fetal embryonic development: a six-week-old embryo already has an articulated mouth, lips, upper and lower jaw. Like a bud opening, our tongue begins to blossom, and twenty milk teeth germinate in our gums. By month four, we can open our mouths and firmly press our lips together. While still in utero, we have managed to assemble all the necessary physiological tools to suck, swallow, root and kiss. At birth we are ready to taste the world.

In mechanical terms, kissing imitates suckling. How does a baby suck? One would imagine that it would be like sipping a milkshake through a straw, but it's not. The anthropologist Desmond Morris, in *Babywatching* (1992), defines the action as "more of squeezing than sucking." It's the pressure of this squeezing action that forces the milk through the engorged nipple, which is deeply inserted into the baby's mouth. This same action is used in a mouth-to-mouth, deep tongue kiss. And it's known that babies will suck for the pure pleasure of sucking, not only for their milk. They also may lick their mothers' nipples with great finesse before the suckling begins.

In his *Three Essays on the Theory of Sexuality* (1905), Sigmund Freud describes the child's private world of thumb-sucking as "a search for some pleasure which has already been experienced and is now remembered." He goes on to explain that the child sucks her thumb to renew the experience of sucking at her mother's breast. Certainly, the warm flow of milk results in a gratifying sensation. The point, though, is that Freud's theory about the "erotogenic zone"—the mouth—has little to do with passion; the satisfaction derived from a mouth kiss is overshadowed, at least for Freud, by "the need for nourishment."

Basic Instinct

Kisses are the messengers of love.
—Danish proverb

Do adults need a variety of oral behaviours to be fully satisfied? Or is it simply that the more sensual objects you put in your mouth—such as a lover's tongue—the more chances there are that some of them will subconsciously mimic the breast? (Psychoanalysts say that men who smoke cigars or pipes do so for the subconscious enjoyment of sucking.) Either way, to kiss and caress another person with the lips and tongue is a basic human instinct. We neither learn—nor forget—how to kiss.

When our lips conjoin in a long kiss, the brain orchestrates lustful feelings and acts as the control centre of our desires. We don't map out exactly where our tongues will explore. We simply go on instinct. The brain tells our lungs to breathe, our hearts to beat faster. As arousal heightens, cardiac rates accelerate from 100 to 175 beats a minute during the plateau phase to 110 to 180+ during orgasm. Blood rushes to the surface of our skin, and we become warmer. We sweat. We are radiant with love flush.

Without question, kissing is the most sensuous type of foreplay. A kiss conveys a feast of data—the type of kiss can determine the disposition of the kisser as well as the state of the relationship. A kiss can pour fresh love from mouth to mouth, and can be more exquisite than the pleasure of an orgasm. Here, the sixteenth-century Dutch writer Johannes Secundus gives us a sublime taste of his beloved's thrilling mouth in "Kiss V" from his book *The Kisses of Johannes Secundus:*

> When you, Neaera, clasp me in your gentle arms, and hang upon my shoulder, leaning over me with your whole neck and bosom, and lascivious face; when putting your lips to mine, you bite me and complain of being bitten again; and dart your tremulous tongue here and there, and sip with your querulous tongue here and there, breathing on me delicious breath . . .

The tongue is overflowing with sensory receptors. This long, tactile organ of interlacing muscles enables extraordinary flexibility and graceful control while kissing deeply. Curiously, the tongue contains most of our ten thousand taste buds on its tiny, nipple-like papillae. This means that a panoply of data is sent rushing to the brain in each savoury nibble. In fact, when we kiss, electrochemical currents rush from the brain along two main nerves that extend fibres to the facial muscles. This explains, in part, why some kisses emit a mild shock. An excellent example of an electric kiss appears in Henry James's (1843–1916) *Portrait of a Lady*: "His kiss was like white lightning, a flash that spread, and spread again, and stayed."

Kissing automatically connects two people. And the more kisses you lavish on your beloved, the more kisses you will receive. The concept is simple: Passionate kisses multiply when they are given. In other words, it is through the exchange of kisses that you gain the skill to kiss each other in a meaningful way and thereby increase your capacity to kiss. An Italian proverb says it best: A kiss once given is never lost.

A romantic kiss is a biological banquet. Exquisitely intimate, our hunger for each other is satisfied only at the endless fountain of sensual nourishment that our mouths provide. We consume each other with every kiss, and with deep kisses it seems we flow into each other's bodies through our lips.

Thousands of years haven't changed the way we kiss. Warm and enduring, reciprocal and enticing, kisses are life-sustaining. They are never-ending. They are full of enchantment. They leave us nourished, breathless, soaring. Kisses kindle the eternal fire of love. They have the power to transform.

Chapter 2

Alchemy of a Kiss

> *Sweet Helen, make me immortal with a kiss.*
> *Her lips suck forth my soul; see where it flies!*
> —*Doctor Faustus,* Christopher Marlowe (1564–1593)

A kiss can be a powerful, transformative elixir. It can change a frog into a prince and awaken a Sleeping Beauty. During the Hindu festival of Nag Panchami in Bishanupur, India, snake charmers bestow a kiss on the throats of venomous cobras to protect their fellow worshippers from danger. The young women of this village believe that puckering up with a cobra will bring them good fortune in wedlock. In Roman Catholic mythology, a kiss applied to the right foot of a saint's statue is thought to restore the sick to health. Kissing is also a mood-altering prophylactic.

When you kiss, chemicals are released in your brain, sending out a rush of positive sensations, lifting your spirits no matter how despondent you are. Even "pretending" a kiss is said to make you feel good.

The anthropologist Desmond Morris describes the curative power of a mother's kiss in his book *Babywatching*:

> Applying [a mother's] lips to the injured spot has no physical or medical value whatsoever, and yet is curiously comforting, both to her and her offspring. This is partly due to the reassuring performance in gentle intimacy, but there is more to it than that. The mother is in fact carrying out an ancient magical practice, symbolically sucking out the "evil forces" that are supposedly causing the pain.

Or perhaps that "ancient medical practice" was itself another elaboration of what has always been a simple, timeless instinct of maternal love: to "kiss and make it better."

Alchemy is one of the most spellbinding words in our language. The term comes from the Arabic *al kimia*—the secret art. A medieval forerunner of chemistry, alchemy sought to transmute base metals into gold through a fusion of science and magic.

Kiss and Tell

You must not kiss and tell.
—*Love for Love*, William Congreve (1670–1729)

While some kisses are destined to soothe, other kisses are imbued with magical powers. For instance, tradition holds that those who kiss the Blarney Stone (the stone set in the wall of Blarney Castle tower, located in the Irish village of Blarney) will be eternally endowed with the gift of persuasive eloquence. The sacred stone is believed to be half of the Stone of Scone (also known as the Stone of Destiny and Jacob's Pillow—which, presumably, has been around since the time of Jacob in the Bible). One medieval legend says that an old woman infused the stone with magical powers to repay a king who had saved her from drowning. Kissing the enchanted stone fortified the king with a suave tongue.

The term *blarney*, meaning to assuage with sweet talk, was coined by Queen Elizabeth I (1533–1603), likely because of her exasperation with the Lord of Blarney's stream of unfulfilled promises to relinquish the castle to the Crown. After kissing the stone, Blarney prolonged his stay by using gentle, manipulative words, which came to be known as "Blarney talk," and later, simply as "Blarney."

Kissing the famed stone is apparently quite a physical challenge. People who kissed the Blarney Stone in Blarney's day were suspended by their heels over the edge of the parapet. Undoubtedly, more than a few hapless souls went hurtling to their deaths by this method. Those desiring to become smooth talkers today must get a local guide to assist them while they lean backwards into the abyss and, grasping the iron rails, lower themselves until their lips are flush with the stone. This is not unlike the upside-down kiss technique performed by Hollywood actor Tobey Maguire in Sam Raimi's action film *Spider-Man* (2002). The rain is teeming down and Spider-Man is hanging upside-down from his webbing when actress Kirsten Dunst shows her gratitude to the super hero for saving her life. She peels down—or rather, up—his mask and covers his mouth, quite fervently, with her own.

Fortune's Kiss

How delicious is the winning
Of a kiss at Love's beginning.
—"Freedom and Love," Thomas Campbell (1777–1844)

The Western custom of kissing under a bough of mistletoe originated among the Druids (priests of ancient Celtic Britain, Ireland and Gaul), who believed in the immortality of the soul and to whom mistletoe was sacred. Their religious ceremonies were performed in oak tree groves—the combination of the oak and the mistletoe (an aerial hemi-parasite that grows on the oak) was thought to possess divine powers. Mistletoe was also thought to promote fertility, probably due to its greenness throughout the year.

In eighteenth-century England, if a woman standing under the mistletoe received a kiss she would marry within the year. If she remained unkissed then she had little prospect of tying the knot. If the two exchanging a kiss were well acquainted it signified a hasty betrothal. And the kiss promised loyalty and prosperity for couples who were already joined. (Those of you who wish to enhance the effects of mistletoe magic should pluck a berry when you kiss the person standing under the mistletoe. But don't attempt to eat it. The waxy, white berries are, ironically, poisonous.)

We also kiss everyday objects out of superstition. According to French beliefs, if you want to have gambler's luck you must kiss your cards before your first play. In Germany, if you make the sign of the cross three times and kiss the ground three times you will protect yourself from being struck by lightning. If you drop a book in Denmark, you must pick it up and kiss it to preserve wisdom.

Body and Soul

> Oh, they loved
> dearly; their souls
> kissed, they kissed
> with their eyes,
> they were both
> but one single
> kiss!
>
> —*Book of Songs*, Heinrich Heine (1797–1856)

A kiss can fuse two bodies into one: Hermaphroditus, the breathtakingly handsome son of Hermes and Aphrodite, was bathing naked when the nymph of the fountain of Salmacis saw him and tried to kiss him. Her advances were spurned, so she prayed to the gods to be forever joined with the beautiful idol. Her request was granted and their bodies merged into one body that displayed both male and female sexual characteristics. This story, of course was intended to explain the rare but puzzling occurrence of ambiguous gender, which is still known today as hermaphroditism.

The matrimonial kiss is also a soul pact, a blissful mingling of identities, a celestial fusion in which two become one. For the early Romans (the first to classify kisses into those between acquaintances, those between friends, and those between lovers), the nuptial kiss (*osculum interveniens*) at the altar was said to symbolize the union of man and woman as they exchanged each other's life essence. Since then, a kiss has been used to seal marriage vows. "One who gives an honest answer gives a kiss on the lips," states Proverbs 24:26. The spiritual note is so intense that one dares not think of this kiss in terms of pleasure. Perhaps this is the reason that, at least traditionally, prostitutes never kiss their clients on the mouth. (Or, is it simply because hygiene is placed before passion? Mouths are known to be filled with more bacteria than clean genital regions.) To the troubadour, a medieval travelling poet and singer, a tender glance and a sacrosanct kiss were equal to the magical bond of intimacy and rapture. Moreover, a troubadour of any stature was expected to feel a satisfying anguish if his beloved did not grant him the kiss. The kiss itself was the ultimate reward.

Here, in a famous passage from *Remembrance of Things Past*, the French writer Marcel Proust (1871–1922) compares the soul kiss of Albertine to receiving communion:

> When it was Albertine's turn to bid me good night, kissing me on either side of my throat, her hair caressed me like a wing of softly bristling feathers. Incomparable as were those two kisses of peace, Albertine slipped into my mouth, making me the gift of her tongue, like a gift of the Holy Spirit.

Fatal Attractions

> *Kisses are the remnants of paradise.*
> —*Nostromo*, Joseph Conrad (1857–1924)

The kiss of Judas has treason at its core and is an eponymous allusion to Judas Iscariot, one of the twelve disciples of Jesus, who in exchange for thirty pieces of silver betrayed Jesus with a kiss of identification to the high priests and elders of Jerusalem. To this day, the name Judas remains synonymous with betrayal. The use of the deceptive kiss to conceal a treacherous act is also found in the Old Testament (Proverbs 27:6): "Better the love that scourges, than hate's false kiss."

The vampire's kiss not only betrays, it drinks its victim's soul. A kind of inverse alchemy, it transforms a kiss of desire into a kiss of death. In Bram Stoker's (1847–1912) *Dracula* (first published 1897), Count Dracula's three female underlings are dazzling and irresistible: "I felt in my heart a wicked burning desire that they would kiss me with those red lips." But their alluring kisses are clearly fatal.

In *The Ballad of Reading Gaol*, the poet and playwright Oscar Wilde (1854–1900) wrote about his love affair with Lord Alfred Douglas (a.k.a. Bosie), for whom Wilde has risked everything, and the deceptive kiss that finally led to his destruction:

And all men kill the thing they love,
By all let this be heard,
Some do it with a bitter look,
Some with a flattering word,
The coward does it with a kiss,
The brave man with his sword!

Stolen Kisses

Stolen sweets are always sweeter
Stolen kisses much completer.
—"Songs of Fairies Robbing an Orchard," Leigh Hunt (1784–1859)

Kisses can even be stolen. In Anton Chekhov's (1860–1904) short story "The Kiss," the love-famished Ryabovich enters into a shadowy room and steals kisses from a lady who secretly awaits her beau. This fleeting act soon flowers in his memory into a frenzy of passion for a woman he will neither kiss nor see again.

Kisses can also be appropriated from one who sleeps. Consider the purloined kisses in *Metamorphoses*, the early myth of Cupid and Psyche, by Lucius Apuleius (A.D. c. 123–c. 170), whereby Psyche presses "ambrosial lips" on Cupid's mouth while he slumbers. Or the most famous of all awakening kisses, *Sleeping Beauty*. This stolen kiss, the apotheosis of fairytale romance and the embodiment of all things

"Giving kisses, stealing kisses, Is the world's chief occupation."
—Ludwig Christoph Heinrich Holty (1748–1776)

chivalrous, is clearly the ultimate male fantasy: the virginal beauty lies waiting to be roused from an enchanted sleep by her prince. The forbidden flavour is intensified because the woman does not partake in, or consent to, the kiss. For the nineteenth-century German poet Heinrich Heine, the most blazing kisses are those that have been seized in dusky secrecy:

> Kisses that one steals in darkness,
> And in darkness then returns—
> How such kisses fire the spirit,
> If with ardent love it burns!

And, a kiss can go beyond the corporeal. The infatuated hero in *The Scarlet Pimpernel*, by Hungarian novelist Baroness Orczy (1865–1947), covers the floor with kisses where his heroine's skirts have swept: ". . . as soon as her light footsteps had died away within the house, he knelt down upon the terrace steps, and in the very madness of love he kissed one by one the places where her small foot had trodden."

In the elaborate formula of love, our deep kisses transform us. We engulf one another. We drink the sweet elixir of each other's desire. Our kisses migrate, they can touch any part of us: fingers, legs, foreheads, shoulders. Kisses make us newly aware of our skin's topography; we are taken, by mouth, across the landscape of our bodies. We drown in a sea of kisses to re-emerge in a sea of passion. Here, in *Euvres de Louize Labé Lionnoize*, the sixteenth-century French poet Louise Labé describes the gorgeous alchemy of kissing:

> Let me gulp your kisses, and you gulp mine,
> And with our mouths sip each other's bliss . . .

Chapter 3

A Panoply of Kisses

The Origins of Desire

> *From the four corners of the earth they come*
> *To kiss this shrine, this mortal-breathing saint.*
> —The Merchant of Venice, William Shakespeare (1564–1616)

Regardless of our world's plurality—despite language barriers and religious differences—most cultures do kiss in one form or another. Some cultures kiss modestly, some kiss ardently, and some kiss violently, sucking and nipping each other's lips. Some cultures don't use their lips at all. The Polynesians, Maori and Inuit, for example, prefer to rub noses. Other cultures, such as the reserved Cayapa Indians of Western Ecuador, simply sniff their friends' hands when greeting. For members of a tribe in New Guinea, the goodbye "kiss" calls for one person to place his hand in a companion's armpit, then rub the scent over himself.

Although the kiss is an almost universal human experience, why we kiss varies from culture to culture. For many, kissing is a pleasurable and appropriate activity, both socially and on more intimate levels. We often kiss to express our recognition and esteem for certain members of our social group. Not only does a kiss confirm our relationship with others, it represents a conduit to deeper feelings.

Kissing, however, is not for everyone. For some tribes, the physical act of kissing is considered unclean. For example, the Thonga of South Africa don't kiss at all—at least, not on the mouth. The mere sight of two people kissing is, in fact, enough to inspire disgust. The Chewa tribe of South Africa, on first seeing Europeans kiss, were repulsed by the thought of "swallowing each other's dirty saliva." Why? For certain tribes, the mouth symbolizes the life source—a place where the soul dwells. Souls can easily become contaminated if one is not careful. Certain African cultures such as the nomadic Mursi and Karo tribes of Ethiopia regard lips as sensual, but they don't necessarily use them for puckering up. They are famous for their traditional lip plates, and while stretched, pierced and mutilated lips may symbolize beauty for many, they can make mouth-to-mouth kisses difficult, if not impossible, to carry out. Some Finnish peoples, whose women and men are accustomed to bathing in the nude together, still view kissing as obscene. Most Asians avoid all forms of kissing in public as it violates their standards of modesty. In Japan, kissing is something you don't want to be caught doing in the street; this very discreet act has its place—in the bedroom. Respectful bows are typically employed as substitutes. Still, for others—including the Maori of New Zealand as well as groups in Borneo and Siberia—the word *kiss* actually means "to smell." For these cultures, the act of kissing is an "exchange of souls"—between friends, relatives or lovers.

Probably one of the most elaborate kisses, at least by Western standards, was recorded in 1929 by Bronislaw Malinowski, the founder of British social anthropology, who was esteemed for his fieldwork method known as "participant observation." He noted that the people of the Trobriand Islands of the South Pacific, a small volcanic island group off southeast New Guinea, part of Papua New Guinea, spent hours in a kind of "savage" nose and mouth play. In *The Sexual Life of Savages*, Malinowski reports:

> Gradually the caress becomes more passionate, and then the mouth is predominantly active; the tongue is sucked, and tongue is rubbed against tongue; they suck each other's lower lips, and the lips will be bitten till blood comes; the saliva is allowed to flow from mouth to mouth. The teeth are used freely, to bite the cheek,

to snap at the nose and chin... In the formulae of love magic, which here as elsewhere abound in over-graphic exaggeration, the expressions "drink my blood" and "pull out my hair" are frequently used... Another element in love making, for which the average European would show even less understanding, [is] the biting off of eyelashes.

The furious mixture of tongue sucking, nose biting, saliva and blood make Western versions of kissing appear much tamer by comparison. We might conclude: a kiss is not just a kiss.

How you kissed in ancient Greece around 300 B.C. depended on your position in society. Those of equal rank might kiss each other on the cheek or mouth, but you kissed those who were more powerful on the hand. In classical Greek art, a person kissed the gods by brushing his fingers to his own lips. (The fingertip kiss as an act of friendship is still practised in present-day Greece.) In Rome in the first century B.C. one also greeted iconic images by kissing one's fingertips and blowing the kiss toward the idol. Roman lovers kissed on the lips, and friends received affectionate pecks on the cheek. A Roman emperor could expect to receive a kiss on the foot.

Kneeling and pressing one's lips to the ground was well-worn kissing practice throughout the Middle Ages (and

> "There is gold, and here / My bluest veins to kiss—a hand that kings / Have lipped, and trembled kissing."
> —*Antony and Cleopatra*, William Shakespeare (1564–1616)

possibly the origin of the phrase "I kiss the ground you walk on"). Even the footprints of kings were venerated with kisses; subjects would literally lick the dust. In *The Thousand and One Nights*, nobles kissed the floor in honour of their sultans.

The ultimate stamp closing on a formal letter in sixteenth-century Spain was QBSP: *Que Besa Su Pies*, "Who kisses your feet." A kiss was also used to seal legal contracts—those who were illiterate would draw an X on the signature line and then kiss it. This would make it a binding contract. The X also symbolized the holy cross, and kissing it implied the declaration of truth.

The holy kiss (*osculum pacis*) is a kiss of devotion. It played an important part in the Roman Catholic Church and is still recognized as a symbol of peace in which the hearts and souls of the faithful are brought together. The concept of souls being exchanged by virtue of breath is evident. Both the mystic quality and unitive function of the holy kiss were expressed succinctly by St. Augustine (A.D. 354–430—one of the foremost philosopher-theologians of early Christianity), who said: "Christians, kiss one another with a holy kiss. It is the sign of peace; as the lips make it known so let it be in our minds." Today, the once-common Catholic ritual of kissing one another with a holy kiss—to signify peace—has been replaced by the handshake, both in Catholic ceremony and in everyday interactions.

> The "soul kiss" (also known as the "sniff-kiss") symbolizes the fusion or union of souls. This intermingling of souls can be found in the Old Testament (Genesis 2:7) when God created man by infusing into his nostrils the "spirit of life." It might even be said that God is Himself (or Herself) the Kiss of Life.

The Church also ritualized the kissing of holy objects such as religious relics, crosses and candles. Priests blessed palms with kisses. The book of the Gospels was devotedly covered in them by both the clergy and parishioners. The faithfuls' reverent lips caressed the hands of the clergy as well as most of the vestments and apparatus associated with the liturgy. Just as Mary Magdalene kissed the feet of Jesus, kissing the feet of a particular saint's statue has led people to go on pilgrimages, and has purportedly healed maladies for centuries. Kissing the cross was thought to bestow eternal happiness. In the absence of a cross, devout Catholics would kiss their thumbs spread in the form of a cross. To "kiss the slipper" refers to kissing the Pope's right slipper, or rather the cross that was embroidered on its toe. It was a common tradition during the Middle Ages for parents to kiss a newborn baby three times in the name of the Holy Trinity. Such divine kisses were believed to help guide one through life, bestowing upon the baby wisdom and everlasting joy.

> "So, break of this last lamenting kiss/Which sucks two souls, and vapours both away."
> —"The Expiration," John Donne (1572–1631)

No kiss can be as poignant as a farewell kiss to the dying, for it takes with it the assurance of future reciprocation. It is the kiss of grief. We part, our beloved's kiss still feverish on our lips. In *Daniel Deronda*, British novelist George Eliot (1819–1880) described it: "That farewell kiss which resembled greeting, that last glance of love which becomes the sharpest pang of sorrow."

In ancient Greece and Rome, delivering the "last kiss" was thought to immortalize a dying person's spirit. Even today people press their lips to the lips of a dying partner, inhaling the final breath, probably in the belief that their death-kiss will stay with the soul throughout eternity.

And some continue to kiss even after death. In Greek mythology, Cyparissus was racked by grief when he accidentally killed his favourite companion, a sacred stag, with his javelin. He beseeched heaven to let his tears and kisses flow for all eternity. His prayers were answered and he was turned into a cypress, the tree of sorrow, so that his gracile boughs will always kiss the earth and wind with his tears.

Kisses have expressed peace, passion and loyalty. And even if certain kisses have been regarded as obscene in some cultures, kisses have remained symbols of devotion. It would be difficult to imagine a world without kissing.

Fire Within: The Erotic Kiss

My desire and thy desire
Twining to a tongue of fire . . .
—"My Delight and Thy Delight," Robert Bridges (1844–1930)

"O embrace now all you millions / With one kiss for all the world."
—"An die Freude," Johann Christoph Friedrich von Schiller (1759–1805)

In the foray of erotic love, lovers' lips signal to each other, and a kiss delivers an urgent message of desire—with a postscript of burning passion. Confident, spontaneous, the erotic kiss bestows a sublime feeling of eternal youth, joy and vigour. We all yearn for such euphoric kisses.

In his essay "The Libation of Three Peaks," Wu Hsien, a Tao of Loving master during the Han Dynasty of 206 B.C.–A.D. 219, details the importance of deep, erotic kissing. To begin, all three peaks—the lips, the breasts and the womb—are vital to the harmony of *Yin* and *Yang*. The highest peak has the male applying sensuous kisses to the female's Red Lotus Peak (lips) and drinking her Jade Fluid (saliva) from the Jade Spring (two holes positioned under the woman's tongue). Taoist alchemy regards saliva as a transporter of vital energies. The second peak involves kissing the female's Twin Peaks (breasts). These ensuing kisses are particularly beneficial to the woman as they relax and open both her Flowery Pool (mouth) and the Palace of Yin (womb)—the third peak.

Indian culture is credited for developing the kiss into an erotic gesture when, about 1,600 years ago, the *Kama Sutra of Vatsayana* was conceived. The classic Indian sex manual, penned by Mallanaga, a monk who belonged to the Vatsayana sect, sometime between the first and fourth centuries A.D., flaunts over thirty styles of kisses. The word *Kama*, from Sanskrit, means sensuous love or desire. *Sutra* is a sonnet-like verse.

The blissful destinations for kisses recommended in the *Kama Sutra of Vatsayana* include the forehead, the cheeks,

> According to ancient Taoist traditions, there is a perfect harmony in our universe. All actions, such as inhaling and exhaling, occur in complementary pairs, and each of these forces—*Yin*, the female force, and *Yang*, the male force—belong to a unique sexual power.

A PANOPLY OF KISSES

the eyes, the throat, the breasts, the navel, the lips and inside the mouth. (The book also details five unique biting kisses as excellent options to divert one's lover.) It goes on to list four categories of kisses—soft, moderate, contracted and pressed—harmonized according to the part of the body being kissed. Of the three kinds of kisses recommended to a young woman—the "nominal kiss," the "touching kiss" and the "throbbing kiss"—only the throbbing kiss comes close to possessing an erotic element: the woman manoeuvres her lower lip against the lip that is pressed into her mouth. If the latter kiss sounds dated, the modern-day "cocoon kiss" is its decadent double. This is achieved by placing your lips around the upper lip of a partner and simultaneously having your amour do the same to your lower lip. Suck gently, nuzzling his lip between your own. Then alternate positions. To enhance the rapturous sensation, slowly envelop his lips with your own. What makes this particular kiss so alluring is that the lips become swollen and sumptuous, making them ultra-erotic.

The *Kama Sutra of Vatsayana* also mentions a hybrid kiss called the "greatly pressed kiss," which is performed by taking hold of a lover's lower lip between two fingers, flicking it with the tongue, and then pinching it gently. A contemporary version of this highly erotic digital-lip squeeze can be found in the "pinch kiss." This time the finger is used to trace the outline of a lover's lips. After a full, slow rotation of the mouth, take his lower lip between your thumb and index finger and gently pinch it into a seductive pucker. For an extra-ecstatic touch, draw the succulent morsel into your mouth.

In addition to these smouldering kisses, the *Kama Sutra of Vatsayana* elaborates on a certain "clasping kiss" (when one of the partners vigorously sucks both the upper and lower lips between his or her own), and the "fighting of the tongue" kiss (involving a tantalizing 360-degree tongue-tour of a lover's mouth interior).

Here are some classified kisses from the *Kama Sutra of Vatsayana*:

> *Passion-kindling kiss:*
> When a woman looks at the face of her lover while he is asleep, and kisses it to show her intention or desire, it is called a "kiss that kindles love."

> *Distracting kiss:*
> When a woman kisses her lover while he is engaged in business, or while he is quarreling with her, or while looking at something else, so that his mind may be turned away, it is called a "kiss that turns away."

> *Awakening kiss:*
> When a lover coming home late at night kisses his beloved who is asleep on her bed, in order to show his

desire, it is called a "kiss that awakens." On such an occasion the woman may pretend to be asleep at the time of her lover's arrival, so that she may know his intention and obtain respect from him.

Purposeful kiss:
When a person kisses the reflection of the person he loves in a mirror, in water or on a wall, it is called a "kiss showing the intention."

Transferred kiss:
When a person kisses a child sitting on his lap, or a picture, image or figure, in the presence of the person beloved by him, it is called a "transferred kiss."

Demonstrative kiss:
When at night at a theater, a man coming up to a woman kisses a finger of her hand if she be standing, or a toe of her foot if she be sitting, or when a woman in shampooing her lover's body places her face on his thigh (as if she were sleepy) so as to inflame his passion, and kisses his thigh or great toe, it is called a "demonstrative kiss."

> *Vatsayana*'s motto: "Whatever things may be done by one of the lovers to the other, the same should be returned by the other; that is, if the woman kisses him he should kiss her in return; if she strikes him he should also strike her in return."

In the seventh century A.D., the Chinese Master Tung-hsuan rigorously outlined in his *Ars Amatoria (Art of Love)* how one should and should not perform the erotic kiss. A lot seemed to depend on whether one was involved with a first-time partner or someone with whom one had an enduring rapport. The former required a diligent application of enticing words, gentle caresses and delicate kisses. For the latter, it was essential that the man's Jade Stalk (a Chinese euphemism for penis—also known as Coral Stem, Red Bird and Heavenly Dragon Pillar) pay homage to the woman's Cinnabar Gate (vulva—also known as the Vermilion Gate, Golden Lotus and the Open Peony Blossom), lingering lightly, while he kissed her Red Lotus Peak (lips), from which the Jade Fountain Liquid (saliva) would flow. Much as in today's Asian cultures, kissing was played out in the very private world of the Jade Chamber (the bedroom), and was never practised publicly.

Passionate couples have been depicted in various art forms (primarily sculpture and painting) for thousands of years throughout India. Some of the most stunningly graphic sexual activities can be found in the stone carvings of the Khajuraho temple, built in central India during the tenth century A.D. (The village of Khajuraho is situated near the town of Kalinjar—once the heart of India's Tantrism—perhaps explaining the highly explicit eroticism of the architecture and the art.) In marvellous, rising tiers of carved figures, the sexual disciplines of Tantra are unveiled in an exquisite abundance of daring postures. Many of the scenes illustrate sexual exercises and techniques such as cunnilingus and fellatio. Some figures are engaged in orgy-like group sex. It was generally believed in India that sex education couldn't be taught in the classroom—it would come naturally through observation and experimentation. Indeed. For motivation there are a number of carvings that exhibit couples entangled in intricate love knots. In one such carving, a sexually aroused couple is shown having coitus while in a standing position. The man has his right foot dexterously clasped around his lover's waist. He kisses her mouth while fondling her breasts and entering her *yoni* (vagina). Another sexually advanced couple is shown in a carnal "wheelbarrow" stance. With her belly pressed to the ground and her legs widely Vee'd over his hips, she gracefully (and painstakingly!) arches her back to grip his hair and hold a passionate kiss.

Sexologists today encourage us all to pick up pointers from our sexually sage ancestors. And an endless series of magazine articles claims that we can all heighten our arousal by adding some oral imagination. When you decide to indulge, try, for example, creating a corporeal buzz by making soft purring sounds while kissing your partner's neck—near an earlobe for best results. The vibrating murmur is said to send jolts of galvanizing pleasure through the recipient's body. A likewise euphonious range of orgasmic sensations can be achieved by varying resonance. Or give each other a mouth-to-mouth version of sizzling sex. To do this, slowly dip your tongue between your lover's slightly parted lips. Next, thrust it seductively in and out.

Similar to the *yoni* (vagina) and the nipples, the lips are one of the major erotogenic zones. In fact, the only other female body part that boasts more nerves and sensitivity is the clitoris. A woman's lips, nipples and clitoris seem to be connected and become charged during an erotic kiss—at least, according to ancient Indian philosophy. The sexual culprit is the subtly curved channel that flexes downward from the nostrils to the mouth—that narrow groove between the upper lip and the nose. This blissful valley realm is called the *nadi*. According to early Indian beliefs, it is credited for creating a direct link for the transmission of energy from a woman's lips to her clitoris (and vice versa), especially while indulging in an opulent kiss. Envision the *nadi* as an oscillating beam of vibrant energy pulsating from the upper lip of the mouth to the clitoris. It's no wonder early erotic texts such as the *Kama Sutra of Vatsayana* highly recommend the nibbling, kissing and biting of the upper lip.

Poets of Gold: The Roman Kiss

> *I should be mad to cover all I could touch with kisses.*
> —*The Love Books of Ovid*, Ovid (43 B.C.–A.D. c. 18)

In first-century Rome, there were three dominant types of kisses: *oscula*, a kiss on the cheek that symbolized friendship; *basia*, a kiss on the lips that represented affection; and *suavia*, a deep, passionate mouth kiss for lovers.

The *jus osculi*—or family kiss—was also popular among Romans. This hybrid of the *oscula* kiss was particularly fashionable because it allowed all of a woman's relations to kiss her. In one of his elegies, Sextus Propertius (c. 54 B.C.–A.D. 2), a great elegiac poet of early Rome, pokes fun at his mistress for fabricating an entire mob of relations so as always to have someone available to kiss her. It is interesting to note that in the mid-sixteenth century, kissing in public was banned in Naples, Rome's nearby sister city. With public kissing deemed blasphemous by the Church, you could spend the rest of your life in prison if caught smooching in the street, or, even worse, face death if the kiss was witnessed by a religious figure.

It seems that romantic love was alive and well in ancient Rome. The poets of the day were so enamoured with the notion of kissing that they would often use the word *kiss* to mean "coitus." Latin erotic literature is known to have existed from the third century B.C., though the first poet whose works survive in fragmented verses is Ennius (c. 239–169 B.C.). Like other Roman writers of his time, Ennius was influenced by the Greeks and Etruscans of several centuries earlier, and he believed that the twelve deities (six female and six male)—Juno, Vesta, Minerva, Ceres, Diana, Venus, Mars, Mercurius, Jovi, Neptunus, Vulcanus and Apollo—were the great instigators of love and delicious intimacies.

Hedonistic pleasure was a central theme among the *Neoterici*, or "New Poets," of the first century B.C., who delighted in sensual literary allusion. It was the daring and original Catullus (87–c. 54 B.C.) who would imprint the Roman love-verse with a spontaneously frank and personalized erotic style. (Catullus was particularly known for his coarse language, which, however superbly glossed, jolts us with abrasive obscenities and assaults on good taste.) Diametric thoughts appear to have played an important role in the poet's core material: "*Odi et amo,*" he wrote. "I love and hate." Nevertheless, he was the first Roman poet to give creative expression to the inner, heartfelt experience of love. Catullus was, like Sappho, one of the world's greatest and most influential love poets. When he was about twenty-six, he had an unrequited affair with the married Clodia Metelli—the "Lesbia" of his poems (apparently named in honour of Sappho, who lived on the island of Lesbos). His famous literary treatment of the kiss celebrates obsessive love in a verse that begins with *"Vivamus / mea Lesbia..."* "Lesbia / Live with me..."

> Kiss me now a
> thousand times &
> now a hundred
> more & then a
> thousand more again
> till with so many
> hundred thousand
> kisses you & I
> shall both lose count
> nor any can
> from envy of
> so much kissing
> put his finger
> on the number
> of sweet kisses
> you of me &
> I of you,
> darling, have had.

"A Skillful lover blends his words with kisses," wrote Ovid (43 B.C.–A.D. c.18) in *Ars Amatoria* (*Art of Love*), a vigorously jocular guide on the art of seduction, although the main objective of the guide seems to be how to delight in a woman's body. This erotic manual promotes a wicked blend of sensuality, humour and explicit sex. The first part of the *Art of Love* teaches the ardent lover how to "win" his mistress, and moves on to instruct this novice "Romeo" how to "retain" her: "Good looks are something, but charm of manner is a great deal more. Pleasant words—like music—are the food of love. Never squabble. Quarrels are the dowry which married folk bring one another. A mistress should only hear agreeable things. This, and all my counsels, are intended for lovers of small or moderate incomes. If a man has got money, there's no need for him to learn the *Art of Love*. Money is the sure passport to a woman's favours. If you are not endowed with wealth, you must make up for it in other ways. Pander to her when she's well; pet her and coddle her when she's sick. Don't make her take nasty medicine, or put her on a lowering diet. Leave that sort of thing to your rival. And don't try to rush things."

Ovid advises would-be seducers to conceal their carnal intentions from their unsuspecting dates, but imposes kisses on women nonetheless with the hope that they will reciprocate:

> What lover of experience does not know how greatly kisses add cogency to tender speeches? If she refuse to be kissed, kiss her all the same. She may struggle to

begin with. "Horrid man!" she'll say; but if she fights, 'twill be a losing battle. Nevertheless, don't be too rough with her and hurt her dainty mouth. Don't give her cause to say that you're a brute. And if, after you've kissed her, you fail to take the rest, you don't deserve even what you've won. What more did you want to come to the fulfillment of your desires?

Ovid's work is at its most dazzling in *Metamorphoses*, a treasure trove of stolen kisses and mythical tales of transformation. "Pygmalion," the love story of a Greek sculptor and his beautiful ivory statue, has a solid eroticism that makes this tale, along with "Echo and Narcissus," one of the most borrowed classics in the arts. In the story, Pygmalion admires his creation so much that he falls hopelessly in love with it. Deeply in denial about her "realness," he often touches her as if to assure himself of her statuesque properties. But it doesn't stop there. Ovid's libidinous chiseller perseveres, "his mind refusing to conceive of it as ivory / he kisses it and feels his kisses are returned." Then, after an interlude of emotional torment,

> . . . he went directly to his image-maid,
> bent over her, and kissed her many times,
> while she was on her couch; and as he kissed,
> she seemed to gather some warmth from his lips.

By now, and much to our protagonist's astonishment, the statue reveals pulsating veins. He pours out a "lavish thanks to Venus; / pressing with his raptured lips / his statue's lips. / Now real, true to life."

In a way, Ovid's kiss is instinctive; it becomes physically mutual as the sensual statue assumes human characteristics. The lover creates his beloved and sees her as he wishes to, not as she is. The fact that Ovid rhapsodizes about the voluptuous statue suggests that attraction exists in the mind, and that the mind can trick the senses.

Gateway to the Soul: The Sniff-Kiss

> *A soft breath issued from our mouth; I felt*
> *It pass through my body and my heart.*
> —Ch'en Meng-Chia (b. 1911)

The sniff-kiss can signify the infusion of a spiritual power—a liaison of souls carried by the breath. Sniff-kissing or nose-rubbing is common among the Inuit (formerly referred to as "Eskimo"—thus the "Eskimo kiss") and the Maori of New Zealand, who greet each other by caressing noses, usually twice. Many Malayan races indulge in the nose-salute (dubbed the "Malay kiss"), and this rubbing form of osculation is widely practised throughout Africa and parts of Asia.

Through nose-to-nose contact, two people exchange

breaths in a sort of airy union. This concept can also be found in Christian theology whereby God infuses the spirit of life into the newly created man by breathing into him (Genesis 2:7). Nicholas Perella, author of *The Kiss: Sacred and Profane* (1901), wrote of the existence of sniff-kissing in parts of Africa, India and Europe (with evidence dating from as early as 2000 B.C.), where two people would bring their faces together in a gesture of spiritual bonding. It was a common East Indian belief, for example, that expired breath was part of the human spirit. An intermingling of the souls was attained by simply bringing one's nose close to that of another. The *honi* is an honorific Polynesian greeting in which individuals press noses together and inhale at the same time. This act is said to represent the exchange of *ha*, the breath of life, and *mana*, spiritual power between two people. The same sort of nose kiss was observed in Madagascar by the French traveller Alfred Grandidier (1836–1921). He wrote in his journals: "The invisible air which is continually being breathed through the lips is to savages, not only, as with us, a sign of life, but it is also an emanation of the soul—its perfume."

There appear to be a number of variations on how to perform the sniff-kiss. Of the Malay kiss, Darwin observed participants who'd place their noses at right angles, then hastily rub them together, the whole affair not lasting longer than a brisk British handshake. (For certain tribes in Malaysia, Borneo, Burma, India and Siberia the words *smell* and *kiss* are synonymous.) Anthropologists have likewise described aboriginal Australian sniff-kisses that consist of a vigorous nose-to-face rubbing. Among a great many African peoples, an initiator will simply push his or her nose against a partner's face and inhale.

And sniff-kisses not only transpire between humans. A large part of our pleasure of keeping domestic pets is their ability to reciprocate our "kisses"—often by a generous sniff-lick (the typical canine approach), or the velvety nose-rub (what felines do when they are fond of one another). As I write, I have a three-month-old kitten that has taken to pressing his nose lovingly against mine.

According to a report by journalist Shana Aborn entitled "The Strangest Breed" (*Ladies' Home Journal*, May 1993), a survey of over four thousand cat and dog owners revealed that 81 percent of cat lovers indulged in kissing their kitties, while 63 percent of dog companions delighted in smooching their pooches. Furthermore, 57 percent of the cat owners and 66 percent of the dog owners surveyed confessed to greeting their pet companions before their partner and children.

How sniff-kisses got started is difficult to say. Many Westerners believe that it is another, more archaic form of a mouth kiss. This is an unlikely hypothesis. Anthropologists believe that the sniff-kiss evolved from the act of smelling someone's face—an early-mammalian survival mechanism—to help interpret their mood and alert them to danger.

Another sniff-kiss theory is based on pre-mastication—the transfer of soft, pre-masticated food from the mouth of the mother into the mouth of her child. In primitive times, the chewed food presumably had a palatable scent. Most industrialized cultures today offer a variety of mushy, flavourful baby foods as a substitute, but pre-mastication has been practised in most cultures throughout history. It is, then, comprehensible how the smell and pre-mastication of food could eventually lead to the maternal sniff- and mouth kiss between a mother and her child. Whatever may be true about the origins of the sniff-greeting, we do know that certain societies prefer to smell—not taste—their loved ones.

Plaisir d'Amour: The French Kiss

> *They grip, they squeeze, their humid tongues they dart*
> *As each would force their way t'other's heart.*
> —On the Nature of Things, Lucretius (99–55 B.C.)

Nothing ignites passion like an exquisite French kiss. The truth about French kissing is that it is as much a taste of sex as a technique. A French kiss is also known as a soul kiss, deep kiss or tongue kiss. It requires mouth-to-mouth contact where the lips of both partners are open and their tongues explore each other's mouths.

Although the French kiss has probably been around since

The power of smell and kissing is revealed in the Old Testament (Genesis 27:27) when Jacob tricks his father, Isaac, who is blind, into giving him his divine blessings with a kiss that was meant for his older brother, Esau. Jacob procures the kiss by donning Esau's clothes, and Isaac "smelled the smell of his garments."

long before the invention of champagne, the English term didn't bubble up until 1923. Britons actually considered it a slang term—probably based on their interpretation of French sexual culture at the time as hedonistic. The French have always been considered (by both Europeans and Americans) to be connoisseurs in the art of love, and, indeed, with more than twenty French words dedicated to the kiss it isn't surprising that they have been credited with originating the practice.

According to Dutch researcher Theodore Hendrik van de Velde (1873–1937), who in 1926 published the extremely popular *Ideal Marriage*, the French kiss acquired its celebrated name from the unmarried Maraichin couples of the Pays de Mont district in Brittany, who would "sometimes for hours, mutually explore and caress the inside of each other's mouths with their tongues as profoundly as possible." Still, the idea of Brittany's village lovers having been the first people to have perfected the deep tongue kiss seems somewhat questionable. Indeed, the erotic kisses of ancient Asia far surpass the European kiss in terms of history and, possibly, technique.

Viewed unfavourably by many Asian and African cultures, the French kiss is planted at the top of the Western foreplay wish list. Many report it as their favourite type of kiss. Not surprisingly, it's the kiss that novice paramours usually stumble upon during their first romantic encoun-

---

Champagne was first developed in the seventeenth century by a monk, Dom Pérignon. The sparkling white wine had its roots in the old French province of Champagne. The tradition of raising a glass of champagne and drinking to the health of a beloved is typically followed by a kiss.

ters. Experimenting with pressure, wetness and tongue control, this kiss allows you to explore new realms, the cosmic kiss that can send you soaring into uncharted sexual stratospheres. At these heights, lips, mouths and tongues can become messengers of love. And what of the after-effects of a delectable deep kiss performed with real *savoir faire*? Perhaps the most passionate description of the aftermath of a French kiss is found in the fevered pages of *Chéri*, composed by the sensual French novelist Colette (1873–1954):

> Her kiss was such that they reeled apart, drunk, deaf, breathless, trembling as if they had just been fighting. She stood up again in front of him, but he did not move from the depths of his chair, and she taunted him under her breath, "Well? . . . Well?"

She stands before him, taunting him, unsure of the effect of her voluptuous kiss. But he quickly assuages her doubts. He opens his arms in a helpless gesture of bliss, and with his head tilted back in ecstacy, and with tears of desire in his eyes, he moans, "I want you."

Note the storm of emotion in the wake of the kiss. It is no accident, perhaps, that the deep kiss inspires an animal-like lust between the lovers. Such intense feelings are most likely instinctive.

Nowadays, the French kiss has been embraced by most of

> "Lovers can live on kisses and cool water."
> —French proverb

the Western world. And it is not uncommon to witness couples probing with their tongues in public displays of affection—kissing as if they had just invented the technique—on park benches, in subway stations, on escalators, in airport lounges and so forth. But not every culture is comfortable with this exhibitionistic form of love. In Venezuela, for example, a tight embrace and a lengthy French kiss in public view could have you arrested. In Malaysia, too, there is a law that bans kissing in dark movie theatres; a French kiss performed there usually results in an exorbitant fine.

Although kissing in public is considered taboo for most Asian cultures, in Banjar Kaja Sesetan (a small village in the southern part of Denpasar, Indonesia), kissing is openly celebrated in an annual festival called *Med-medan*. Following a rhythmic beat, separate groups of teenaged boys and girls walk in an ellipse pattern until they finally come face to face. Then, the first person in each group kisses the one opposite. After this, an elder pours water over the kissing pairs and the groups divide. The ritual is repeated until all of the young participants have had a chance to be the first person. The objective of this ceremonial "soul kiss" (a hybrid French kiss) is to protect the village from any unforeseen danger. And only if you are a member of the Banjar Kaja Sesetan can you partake in this enthralling ritual.

There are only two major requirements for a French

> Perhaps the most embarrassing faux pas that a foreigner can make is mistranslating the French word *baiser*. Used as a noun, *baiser* means a kiss. But when the innocent-sounding *baiser* is used as a verb, it radically changes meaning—in English it becomes the slang verb "to fornicate."

kiss—lips and tongue. Your lips should be slightly parted and your tongue ready to explore. Chances are, you will instinctively tilt your head slightly so that you don't bump noses. (Lovers' noses usually touch the cheek of the person they are kissing.) Some people enjoy moving their mouths in a spherical motion or a figure eight. The thing to remember is that everyone approaches the subject of kissing differently, and everyone's kisses are unique.

French kissing should always be deliciously light and spontaneous, and intensify as you get caught up in the moment. Try to make each kiss last for three minutes and build up to a kissing session that lasts for an hour. Let your tongue dance, tease and plunge deeply into the very essence of your partner's soul. And keep in mind: an intense kissing session should never conclude in an abrupt manner—the final kiss should always be soft and tender.

The neck and ears are ultra-erogenous zones where the caress of a tongue enkindles exquisite sensations.

Paying Court: The Social Kiss

> *A hand is to be kissed with reverence,*
> *The forehead—solemnly, with friendship,*
> *The cheeks—with tender admiration,*
> *And the lips be kissed with ardour,*
> *While the eyes one kisses with languor,*
> *The neck—with passionate desire,*
> *And with maddening delirium*
> *All the rest is to be kissed.*
> —*A Kiss*, Franz Grillparzer (1791–1872)

The hand-kiss is a courtly form of greeting and almost always carries a sexual connotation, even though the kiss is placed on the back of the hand and not the mouth. Done correctly, it is performed on a subtly bended knee, the gallant cavalier leaning forward to kiss the outstretched hand of the lady.

People have been kissing the hands of the powerful for thousands of years. Students in ancient Greece brushed their lips to their teachers' fingertips. Roman slaves kissed the hands of their masters. But the hand-kiss greeting as we know it today was first practised by the Vikings (eighth to tenth century), whose custom it was to "hand-a-gift" to their Nordic liege lords. From this emerged the "hand-kiss." (When the lord was away, the vassal was expected to press his lips to his door, lock or bolt. In turn, kissing each of these objects was awarded the title: the door-kiss, the lock-kiss and the bolt-kiss.)

Contrarily, a handshake greeting without the kiss tends to be a very firm squeeze, with a single up-and-down motion that conveys a direct frankness. A slack hand, of course, inspires suspicion. The old European handshake does not share the hardy time-is-money shake of the American style. It is instead a warm grasp in which each person in turn brings the other's hand in contact with his chest—where the heart resides. The touch symbolizes sincerity and steadfastness. To reinforce the veracity of this greeting, both hands are offered and affectionately clasped to one's heart. Handshaking between young and old Muslims is a centuries-old form of salutation and is still practised today by some. This respectful greeting involves the younger of the two bowing down to the level of the elder's hand and kissing it. During Hari Raya Puasa (a religious celebration that marks the end of the fasting month of Ramadan), the younger has to bow down on both knees, kiss the hand of the seated elder and ask forgiveness for any wrongdoings.

Today's ever-changing pop culture is the main reason for the proliferation of stylized salutations. Take, for example, the "pound" greeting (borrowed from African Americans). The pound begins with a pair of hands in a thumb-wrestling position, then moves into a mutual finger-snap (that can

> For a seductive variation on the classic hand-kiss: turn your hand over and offer your palm or wrist to be kissed. This gesture requires a great deal of confidence on the woman's part and implies a desire for a more intimate acquaintanceship.

mimic the sound of a kiss smack) prior to releasing. Knuckle-to-knuckle congratulatory "kisses" are big with professional athletes, and appear to have replaced the former "high-five" gesture.

Women and men everywhere can be seen engaging in another form of social kiss—the ever-so-chic and frivolous air-kiss, the successful export of the double cheek-to-cheek kisses that originated in Europe. This theatrical kissing style can be witnessed breezing through cafés, galleries, airports, restaurants, offices, boutiques, cinemas, sidewalks—wherever people mingle and meet. During a social air-kiss the lips never quite touch the cheeks. Nor is there cheek-to-cheek contact. And while this European ritual greeting requires a double kiss, North Americans will often smack their lips in the vicinity of one cheek. According to stylish trend-setters, the practice of the social air-kiss by non-Europeans may have something to do with the Milan fashion scene. They claim that the air-kiss greeting is a remnant of the mid-eighties, when North American buyers and editorial fashionistas were seduced by flamboyant designers and the Mediterranean way of doing things. The outcome? A barrage of *baci* (Italian for kisses). I know from experience (having worked with the fashion icon Gianni Versace in the mid-1980s) that when it comes to model salutations, almost anything melodramatic goes. Anything, that is, but a single soulless kiss. This explains why fashion (and entertainment) industry events are often referred to as "huggy-huggy, kissy-kissy" affairs. A fear of transmittable diseases has also aided in promoting the popularity of the social air-kiss in big cities. This kiss of caution can be performed by positioning your cheeks in close proximity to another's cheeks, without actually touching. Often participants will feign kissing noises, or they will simply say, "Kiss, kiss."

Although the exuberant double kiss is a prerequisite for the classic Italian coterie, it won't suffice if you happen to be greeting the Dutch, Swiss or Belgian chic set. They are all triple kissers by tradition. Encounters with these nationalities can be confusing, and first-timers may think that they are done after the second cheek kiss, only to have their faces held firmly for a flourishing third-kiss finale. Dilettantes usually end up knocking heads or bumping noses trying to figure out which cheek to begin with.

Not sure where to begin? One kiss, two or three? To embrace or not to embrace? Contact or no contact? Shake hands or crisply smile? Social and professional protocol in urban centres today can mean a plethora of confusing, and often conflicting, greeting rituals. Business professionals, in particular, are faced with the dilemma of whether to kiss or shake hands. Some people exchange kisses as bounteously as handshakes. Still, most decorum experts agree that corporate kissing is a faux pas. The kissing controversy has erupted partly because no one, it seems, can agree on an appropriate global business greeting. Many unwary recipients of corporate kisses are left feeling uneasy. Still others contest that the corporate kiss need not feel compromising as it has become simply another form of the handshake.

Those seeking advice need not turn to first-century A.D. Greek poet Nikarchos, whose tongue was in his own cheek when he suggested:

> If you kiss me you hate me; if you hate me
> you kiss me,
> but if you don't hate me, my sweet friend,
> don't kiss me.

How often you encounter corporate kissing depends largely on your environment. Chances are, if you work in an art gallery, restaurant, upscale retail store, public relations firm or luxury hotel, you'll be inundated with kisses. Kissing rarely seems to transpire in lawyers' offices or investment banking establishments. Corporate kissing among male colleagues is scarce in northern Europe, but common in Mediterranean countries such as Spain, Greece and Italy.

With so much diversity, it's no wonder jet-setters get their signals mixed up. They may go from a morning meeting with a group of reserved Japanese associates, to an afternoon conference with aggressive American clients, to an evening *aperitivo* with gregarious Italian neighbours. Needless to say, the line between a perfunctory professional kiss with a perfect stranger and an overzealous dive for some lip action can get smudgy.

Only one thing is certain: the corporate kiss is something no two people perform alike. Ditto for the ceremonial kiss. It is common for heads of state or other dignitaries, particularly in European countries, to bestow a ceremonial kiss upon meeting. This type of kiss is usually of the double-cheek variety and is applied hastily. The ceremonial greeting functions as a powerful political symbol rather than social ritual and it usually conveys the participants' integrity and goodwill.

Prima Materia: The First Kiss

A long, long, kiss, — a kiss of youth, and love.
—*Don Juan*, George Gordon, Lord Byron (1788–1824)

The first kiss can set the stage for the rest of the relationship. Innocent, sexy, light and passionate, it causes participants to soar to erotic heights, and is usually performed while they are fully dressed. Love is often kindled by a first kiss.

Although a well-executed smooch certainly carries the potential to bring two strangers closer together, an ideal

> To kiss or not to kiss? What should you do if someone disagreeable makes a move for your lips? Turn your face and offer them your cheek. You can return the social gesture with a simple peck on their cheek.

first kiss is generally one exchanged between partners who are familiar with each other—the anticipation and longing heighten the experience. When lovers' lips meet for the first time, they kiss with all of their senses, absorbing each other's unique taste and fragrance. The lips, the tongue and the breath are the protagonists of our most sensual moments. It is no wonder that our first romantic kiss invokes a curtain call in our memory. And a first kiss can prompt memories of other first kisses.

One of the most sentimental descriptions of a first kiss is to be found in Victor Hugo's nineteenth-century masterpiece, *Les Misérables*:

> How did it happen that their lips came together? How does it happen that birds sing, that snow melts, that the rose unfolds, that the dawn whitens behind the stark shapes of trees on the quivering summit of the hill? A kiss, and all was said.

It is through our first romantic kisses that a taste of "heaven" comes to us. I experienced my first romantic kiss when I was ten. I was one of the fortunate few who had an eligible beau living right next door to me. Michael was two months my junior, so that made me the "teacher." We lived in Toronto on a hilly street that ribboned high above the steely cold span of Lake Ontario. In the summer our adjoining gardens were urgent with the scent of irises, roses, peonies, delphiniums, asters, violets, and a large honeysuckle vine that fluttered a curtain of fragrance between the two houses.

I remember some details from that mid-August day: Me vainly trying to hang up sheets for my mother that were already flapping like sails in the fiery breeze. Blunt blades of sheared grass prickling my toes. A keen urge to try something new—a new game perhaps. The telephone call to Michael: "Meet me on the top branch of our favourite climbing tree—four o'clock sharp!" The rendezvous apple tree looked as tall to me as a tower. My date was faithfully waiting, perched high amidst the heavy green fruit. Kaleidoscopic leaks of sunlight burst through leaves as I climbed to meet him. And without a word I planted my lips on his, and we kissed. When it was over we scurried down the trunk, seeing who could reach the ground first. He did. Then, gallantly extending his hand upward, he smiled and said, "I love you." I smiled back, the hum of cicadas still ringing in my ears.

As I ran up the path to my house, the world seemed electric; giant dragonflies vibrated prismatic glass wings on day lilies and the mesh on the screen door was alive and magnetic. Everything pulsed with an intimate knowledge.

Praised for his corpus of over five hundred love songs, the fifteenth-century East Indian poet Vidyapati was obviously familiar with the thrilling sensations of a first kiss when he wrote in "First Love":

> Now she has known first love,
> desire floods her mind,
> she trembles with delight.
> . . . she studies her reflection in a jewel.
> knits her brow, and oh
> so tenderly
> touches the blossoming
> love-bite on her lip.

A premier kiss can communicate attraction, affection, passion, love. Many women, myself included, will decide whether or not to have sex with a man based on his initial smooching skills. A mediocre kisser usually won't get past the doorstep. What exactly determines an exemplary kisser? The ideal kisser views the kiss as the ultimate destination, and not the first move on a corporeal mission. Accomplished kissers savour every moment. Sensational first kisses are those that leave partners thirsting for more.

We all possess an exclusive talent to kiss—a unique way of expressing our love. This means that there is at least one kiss that only you can perform better than anyone else in

According to the twelfth-century Latin text The Emerald Tablet, Prima Materia—*or* First Matter—*represents the divine spirit flowing from the depth of a pure and sincere heart.*

this world. When a first kiss is motivated by passion, lovers' lips are sealed by the energy of their desire.

First kisses are the most erotic type of foreplay around, and perhaps the most overpowering. They provide us with our first delicious sip of sex, and allow us to experience all the excitement, adventure, mystery and magic of love.

Seal of Solomon: The Matrimonial Kiss

> *We will have rings and things, and fine array*
> *And kiss me, Kate, we will be married o' Sunday*
> —*The Taming of the Shrew*, William Shakespeare (1564–1616)

"You may now kiss the bride." How many times have we heard this conclusion to the marriage pact? But in order to fully understand where the custom of kissing the bride began, we must first look at the evolution of marriage.

According to anthropologists, the first marriages may have been communal—marriage to the tribe. It can be said with some certainty that our ancestors were more concerned with the protection and the propagation of the clan than they were with building meaningful relationships with significant others. Fidelity, however, must have played an important role as it encouraged pairs to bond and thus ensure the survival of their progeny. Continuous female sexual receptivity (the ability to copulate throughout the cycle, not only during ovulation) likewise promoted pair bonding, or the primeval marriage, as it required males to mate with females on an ongoing basis.

The betrothal kiss (*osculum interveniens*) originated in early Rome. The kiss was regarded as a prelude to matrimonial cohabitation. The earliest record of this type of kiss is by the Christian theologian Tertullian (born Quintus Septimius Florens Tertullianus, c. 160–c. 240), who speaks of the betrothal kiss bestowed on pagan women and their "intermingling with a male body and spirit by way of the kiss and the squeeze of the right hand." The engagement kiss furnished the woman with juridical rights, under the ordinance of the Empire, and the failure of either party to follow through with marriage carried dire consequences. In addition, if a kiss was exchanged at the betrothal, the wedding presents legally belonged to the engaged couple. But if no kiss transpired and one of the promised died before the marriage, then all the gifts had to be returned. (Before the legal sanction of the betrothal kiss, a suspicious Roman might press his lips on his mistress's to ascertain if she had been drinking wine—an illegal activity for women of the first centuries A.D.) The kiss, an obvious symbolic transference of "souls," was eventually incorporated into the Christian marriage ceremony.

There were three forms of marriage that Roman couples

In alchemical terms, the Seal of Solomon, a six-pointed star made by two equilateral triangles, symbolizes the marriage of heaven and earth. It is the harmonization of all elements, the union of opposites—two become one.

The belief that health and happiness came to those who sealed their conjugal vows with a kiss in June—the most popular month for weddings—goes back to the days of early Rome, when Juno, wife of Jupiter and goddess of marriage, was especially honoured.

could choose from: *coemptio*, which was similar to a modern civil ceremony; *confarreatio*, which resembled a ritualistic Catholic church wedding today; and *usus*, a kind of common-law arrangement that was legally binding after a year's continuous rapport. In all three forms, the bride was passed *in manum*—in [to] his hand—from her father's safekeeping into that of her husband. These prototype conjugal patterns, established by the Romans over two thousand years ago, endured in Asia, Europe, Africa and the Americas with minimal cultural variation over the centuries. They continue to serve as blueprints for relationships today.

It wasn't until the sixteenth century, in England, that the wedding feast was celebrated publicly and all the guests were allowed to kiss the bride on the mouth as she posed in the matrimonial bed, clad only in her finest undergarments. These collective kisses were followed by congratulatory speeches and toasts.

Wedding guests attending banquets in seventeenth-century England challenged newlyweds by erecting a stack of round cakes over which the bride and groom had to kiss. This neck-straining kiss was thought to symbolize a happy marriage and prosperity. Not long after, the "kiss of the chimney sweep" was added to the British bride's trousseau. As the title suggests, it involved finding a chimey sweep to kiss the bride on her wedding day. This kiss, too, was thought to impart wealth and marital bliss. Nowadays, an

English bride has only to look at an authentic chimney sweep on her big day in order to reap good fortune.

And what role does the kiss play after the bride and groom say "I do"? When you've been living with the same partner for years, familiarity can dull the delicious, forbidden feelings of early romance. Furthermore, quotidian stresses of work and parenting—not to mention fatigue—can drive away passion and ward off kisses. The good news? Locking lips with your partner not only soothes, but helps you to reconnect as lovers. And because the kissing is pleasurable and not just a fast lane to intercourse, married couples can easily recapture the thrill of kissing anytime they want.

As Above, So Below: The Genital Kiss

Hug me, kiss me, suck my juices
—"Goblin Market," Christina Rossetti (1830–1894)

Few pleasures are as intense as genitalia kisses. These erotically drenched caresses have, for centuries, embodied divine human energy. In the Tantric tradition, such genitalia worship typically involved both genders, but it was the female *yoni* (vagina) that was regarded as a symbol of cosmic mysteries—the universal womb. (*Yoni* is a Sanskrit term that means "origin" and "source.") So a man intent on longevity would make it his goal to absorb as much

---

Here are three benefits of kissing long after the honeymoon is over:

1) Deep kissing short-circuits pent-up stress. Making out with your spouse is said to spark mood-elevating endorphins, which can help prevent bedroom doldrums.

2) Locking lips with a partner is thought to boost your immune system. The exchange of germs can strengthen couples' internal defence systems considerably.

3) Sizzling smooch sessions help tone the underlying muscles of your face and neck, keeping you looking youthful.

female essence as possible. Hence, the mutually gratifying *cunnilingus* (the Latin term for licking, kissing or sucking the *cunnus*, or vulva).

The use of the mouth for cunnilingus or fellatio is a titillating practice that engages the same mouth action used in kissing. For some, kissing another's genitals is a gesture of intimacy that transcends copulation. And, naturally, oral sex well performed can get the juices flowing to the point of orgasm.

The Perfumed Garden (written by Sheik Shaykh Nefwazi of Tunis in the early-sixteenth century and then translated by Sir Richard Burton in 1886) features an exhilarating array of over forty names to celebrate the vulva, among which are the Passage, Starling, Arch, Crested One, Warmer, and Delicious One. The male "virile member" gets equal treatment with such distinguishing sobriquets as Exciter, Quencher, Path Maker, Searcher, Tailor and Discoverer. Genital exploration is encouraged throughout this lovemaking manual, with an emphasis on an array of tender kisses and gentle caresses.

As you begin to experience the transcendence of mouth-to-genital kisses, you become more intimate with each caress. You feel a sparkle, a glow, a burst of pure ecstasy. When you kiss, your lips swell and become more protuberant. Yearning glows along their every millimetre. Your genitals begin to tingle. If you are a woman, your labia minora

The alchemical dictum "as above, so below" implies that those who can understand the ways of heaven will also understand the ways of Earth. Similarly, the deep mouth-to-mouth kiss can be just as pleasurable when experienced below.

also swell and open. If you are a man, your penis becomes engorged and erect. Both sets of lips on the woman's body, as well as the man's, become deep crimson like pomegranate blossoms.

Anthropologists say that women may lick their lips as an unconscious way of reminding men of their other lips—the labia. With a kiss, passionate messages are sent to the brain to rush blood to the genitals, change muscle tension and increase skin sensitivity. As sexual arousal increases in females, the outer lips of the vulva open, but the inner lips enlarge to at least twice their original size in diameter.

Vivid colour changes develop in the embellished lips of this other "mouth." Like summer fruit these colours can range from the coral of watermelons to the glossy red of Montmorency cherries and the wine tint of Tuscan grapes. Whether we are conscious of it or not, labial awareness is said to account for the vast array of women's lipstick hues found in department stores, and for the enormous popularity of today's swollen "bee-stung" lips. Lipstick colours range from sumptuous rosebud shades to the luscious hues of strawberries, cherries, peaches and blackberries. At their most elaborate, lacquered lips are the living, talking, moving, breathing advertisements of one's sensuality. A lavishly painted mouth seems to announce, "Pucker up, I'm ready."

In the animal world, similarly blatant displays of sexual

exuberance signal to the male that the female is ripe for coitus. But females in heat are not the only promoters of sexual pluck. For example, the brilliantly coloured male mandrill, largest of the monkey family found in the tropical forests of Gabon, features a rear end in hues from deep magenta, reds and pinks to lilac blues (the only mammal to possess blue pigmentation). A shocking red and blue muzzle, a yellow "beard" and large canines complete the dashing look. It is clearly the male of this rare species that advertises his readiness to mate. His dramatic colours brighten, due to a surge of testosterone, when he is excited: his rump becomes an electric blue, and red spots frequently appear like neon bracelets on his ankles and wrists. When the female mandrill is ready to mate, a comparatively modest rosy-pink swelling appears around her tail.

The Nuba of Kau, a passionate people who live nestled among the red, dusty rocks of Kadugli, a small Sudanese town in Africa, enjoy visually stimulating genital "kisses" during the mating ceremony of their virginal girls. The *nyertum*, or "dance of love," opens with a frenzy of drums. Slender girls, their long limbs glistening with oil and an explosion of ostrich plumes, swirl naked in the sunlight. An arena of "fighters" sits on low stone walls, waiting to be approached. After a climax of vigorous movement, a girl sways up to her favourite fighter, swings one leg over his head and wraps it around his shoulder. The drums continue to throb as she visually "kisses" her new partner's face with her exposed labia, while at the same time displaying her sexual availability. The partners then move to the bridal hut to consummate what they have suggested throughout the ritual. The mating dance is not unlike the high-kicking Parisian cancan with its symbolic show of ruffled genitalia or the flashy festivals of Mardi Gras and Canadian Caribana, which all possess an air of erotic liberty.

Still, for many men it's difficult not to have performance anxiety about kissing a woman's genitalia. For the gender lacking a clitoris, oral sex is hardly intuitive. (The same can be said of women's oral-sex anxiety over penises.) Nothing, of course, beats the increasingly louder moans and groans elicited when a man (or a woman) is headed in the right direction with oral caresses. One thing is certain, the more a man *thinks* that a woman is being pleasured, the more spontaneous his kisses and the better his technique. (Likewise, a woman should learn to relax her mouth when going "downtown" on a man.)

For the erogenous aficionado, the lips and the tongue mimic both the vulva and the phallus. This means that you can not only experience erotic, genital androgyny but also enjoy a myriad of earth-shaking kisses without the time constraints often associated with coitus. For partners concerned with "coming together," mutual genital caressing using the dual "sex organs" (lips and tongue) can be particularly agree-

---

When I talk with a male friend about kissing a woman "down there," he turns serious. He believes that a lot of men have trepidations about giving oral sex. "What men worry about most," he says, "is how much their partner is going to enjoy being kissed south of the border. It helps if a woman tells you how she really feels about it." I learn that there are certain men, like my friend, who delight in plunging into the depths below with their tongue, lips and teeth. He offers, "I love to linger with my tongue and let the aahs guide me."

able as it allows partners to synchronize their moments of orgasmic bliss.

Cultural beliefs about oral sex vary widely. Male vulvaphobia is prevalent among the Northern Athabascans of Alaska, who, as children, are taught that the vagina is dangerous. For the Mehinaku tribe of the Amazon, a woman's mouth and vagina are equated. In contrast, the Kagwahiv, another Amazonian tribe, enjoy an intensity of passion in which genital kissing between heterosexual couples is freely practised. And the Mangaians of Polynesia not only partake in an extraordinarily active sex life (many young people will have had up to seventy lovers before they are twenty), but also believe that abstinence from sex will cause illness. Erotic technique is held in high esteem by most Mangaian lovers, and erogenous kissing performed with skill is considered godlike.

Chapter 4
Kissing and the Five Senses

The Look of Love

> *Many a kiss, both odd and even;*
> *Many a glance, too, has been sent*
> *From out the eye, love's firmament—*
> —"Corinna's Going a-Maying," Robert Herrick (1591–1674)

It all begins with the eyes, "those silent tongues of love," wrote the visionary Spanish author of *Don Quixote*, Miguel de Cervantes (1547–1616). We are all mesmerized by eyes. From birth we recognize faces, particularly eyes, and as we mature we learn to create intimate bonds through eye contact. In his *Elegies, Book II*, the Roman poet Propertius (c. 54 B.C.–A.D. 2) describes optical passion: "Eyes open—kissing blind's no fun—/ Love feasts eyes first, then lips and tongue."

A kiss is a highly visual action. Lovers usually keep their eyes open when they kiss so that they can drink in each other's faces. Our pupils dilate spontaneously when we are aroused (as do women's cervixes). Enlarged pupils signal sexual interest to a potential lover. And with 70 percent of our sense receptors located in the eyes, visual stimuli play an important role in the way we love. To "give someone the eye" is a flirtatious example of this ocular phenomenon.

In "Song to Celia," British dramatist and poet Ben Jonson (1573–1637) celebrates visual eroticism:

> Drink to me only with thine eyes,
> And I will pledge with mine;
> Or leave a kiss but in the cup
> And I'll not look for wine.

Staring deeply into each other's eyes seems to provoke an immediate reaction. Studies indicate that the pupils of men's eyes dilate as much as 30 percent when viewing photographs of winsome women whose pupils are dilated. The "mating" gaze sparks a part of the human brain that is able to distinguish between the two primitive emotions—advance or retreat. We cannot help but be transfixed by a set of enlarged dark pupils fixed on us. We must respond. "Who ever loved that loved not at first sight," wrote Christopher Marlowe (1564–1593) in *Hero and Leander*. And here

> ". . . each other's dark eyes darting light / Into each other—and beholding this, / Their lips drew near, and clung in a kiss . . ."
> —*Don Juan*, George Gordon, Lord Byron (1788–1824)

Lawrence Durrell (1912–1990) confides the compelling visual power of a kiss in his novel *Justine*: "We lay eye to eye for a long time, our bodies touching, hardly communicating more than the animal lassitude of the vanishing afternoon." After the lovers are finally sated they embrace and begin to kiss with a renewed passion, an ardor enhanced by the love they have enkindled visually.

Eye language was well known to the courtesans of the Italian Renaissance, who would drop poisonous belladonna (meaning "beautiful woman"), from the nightshade family, into their eyes to enlarge their pupils, thus enhancing their desirability to clients. On the other hand, many predators' dagger-shaped pupils are vertical.

Optical movements, lid positions and pupil size all say a lot about what we are feeling. Our pupils (*palpebral fissures*) widen automatically when we are excited, and contract when we are apprehensive. (Rapid eyelid closure reflects an inherited mammalian protective trait that is brought on by the "startle reflex." Widely opened eyes reveal the fight-or-flight response.) We are continually probing each other's eyes for change in mood. Indeed, peering into someone else's eyes is not unlike getting a glimpse of the brain itself, thanks to the nerve endings that cover the retina of our eye that are themselves a physical extension of the cortex. In a sense, the eye's sensory cells "caress" the outside world. Lascivious emotions are displayed in a direct gaze, opened

> "Golden slumbers kiss your eyes,/Smiles awake you when you rise."
> —"The Pleasant Comedy of Patient Grissell," Thomas Dekker (1572–1632)

eyelids and dilated pupils. Potential kissing partners possess an astounding ability to gauge each other's intentions by simply gazing into the eyes. "A lover's eyes will gaze an eagle blind," wrote Shakespeare in praise of ocular infatuation in *Love's Labours Lost*. (But don't overdo it—being stared at can stimulate the sympathetic nervous system to such an extreme that we often end up feeling uncomfortable and compelled to glance away.)

"But to see her, was to love her; / Love but her, and love for ever," the Scottish poet Robert Burns (1759–1796) recorded in "Ae Fond Kiss." Just looking at a lover's lips can send a series of electrochemical messages reeling to the visual cortex of the brain in a tempest of sensory activity. We see in extraordinary detail. And it takes us only a tenth of a second to decode a set of moist pre-kiss lips.

> Eyelash kisses should never be overlooked. A light fluttering of your lashes on your lover's face and neck—known as a butterfly kiss—can add a sexy nuance. Tease, tickle and titillate using feathery, sweeping strokes.

Smiling

> *She smiled, and then, with all her heart and soul,*
> *gave me a kiss, and never was kiss more sweet.*
> —The Love Book of Ovid, Ovid (43 B.C.–A.D. c. 18)

It seems we were born to smile. Studies show that some infants will imitate their mother's smile within two days of birth. Most babies have a repertoire of smiles by three months of age. Desmond Morris, author of *Babywatching*, reports on the "reflex smile"—a smile that involves the whole face and lasts longer than the ephemeral curve of the lips that newborn babies give in reply to the *coo* of an amicable stranger. This effervescent reflex smile, which occurs at about four months of age, is said to be a more specific response to stimuli, such as seeing a parent. Why do babies smile so much? Many social anthropologists believe that the reflex smile makes infants more winsome, and therefore more apt to be protected. Even blind children, who have never seen a smile, beam joyfully.

How we make and interpret the transitory, microsecond expressions that flit across people's faces thousands of times each day is as vital to our cognitive state of well-being as it is to our amorous interactions. With forty-four muscles, with blood vessels and nerves laced through a framework of cartilage and bone all covered by a layer of smooth, pliant skin, the face can push, pull and contort into an astounding five thousand expressions. And, according to anthropologists, humans have at least eighteen unique types of smiles, each employing slightly different combinations of facial muscles.

The smile is the most recognizable and communicable gesture in the world. Smiles guide our fantasies. They connect us. The "open smile" is probably the most enticing human courting stratagem. With lips drawn upward (engaging the zygomatic muscles, which run from the cheekbone to the corners of the mouth, and the *orbicularis oculi*, which create the delightful crinkle in the outer corner of the eye), the upper and lower teeth are fully exposed. The smile is also the least complicated facial expression to execute. Compared to the ninety-six nuances of anger, which depend on several hundred different muscle combinations, smiling is a breezy act. You simply cannot overlook a fully exposed smile: actor Cameron Diaz's dazzling smile is an extraordinary example. For the Japanese, the very word for "smile" is multifaceted and steeped with meaning: *niko-niko*, a smile of tranquility; *ni*, a fleeting grin; and *ninmari*, a smirk.

Can smiles mislead us? Absolutely. By observing opposite-gender couples in casual conversations at bars, anthropologists have been able to synopsize sexual response to smiling. Many women will try to radiate warm smiles to encourage men to talk to them—the smile suggests

"There is a smile of love / And there is a smile of deceit / And there is a smile of smiles / In which these two smiles meet."

—"The Smile," William Blake (1757–1827)

approachability and openness. Men, though, may misinterpret the amicable signal and read it as an invitation to more carnal liaisons. As to why this particular smile should excite us, well, the opened-mouth grimace is a natural response when experiencing elevated sexual stimulation—for example, during the plateau phase or orgasm. Furthermore, an exuberant smile is capable of communicating at great distances, more than any other facial expression; we can pick up a lover's smile at about 90 metres (approximately the length of two city blocks). The "upper smile" is also alluring—it involves exhibiting your upper teeth to demonstrate your good intentions. Interestingly, gorillas and chimps use a "lower smile" when they play, exposing only their bottom teeth so as not to threaten one another with their saber-like upper canine teeth. Humans bare their teeth when feeling cornered or when caught in a socially tight spot. This "nervous smile" stems from an ancient mammalian practice. Predictably, the uptight grin is not likely to lead to an ambush of kisses.

While we may think that smiles and romantic parlances are the best way to get our love messages across, in fact the subliminal vocabulary of our lips can speak volumes.

Leonardo da Vinci's masterpiece *Mona Lisa* features one of the most talked-about smiles in history. Is it the eloquent smile signalling to a secret lover? Is it the smouldering smile of sublime delight, spellbinding as it teases our imagination? Is it the nostalgic smile of remembered kisses? Is it perhaps the smile of conception's bliss?

Lip Logistics

> *Come, gently steal my lips along,*
> *And let your lips in murmurs move.*
> —"The Kiss," Thomas Moore (1779–1852)

Like eyes, lips reveal telling clues about our innermost feelings. Our lips are used to pronounce words, to express emotions and, of course, to kiss. Lips are the most emotionally expressive part of our body. Because our lips are connected to the visceral nervous system and to the companion muscles that surround our mouth, we actually have difficulty keeping them still.

No two pairs of lips are alike. And, even if we know from *Gray's Anatomy* that the lips consist of two *orbicularis orbis* muscles, a kiss is not simply the contraction of these twin puffs. The lips are rife with touch sensors. They are one of the most sensitive areas of our body and, perhaps, the most vulnerable.

The lip lick is the most common non-verbal pickup cue. Some people indulge in only a single, moistening lick, wetting the lower or upper lip, while others slowly glide the tongue over the entire lip zone. It is interesting to note that an extraordinarily generous part of the brain's surface area is devoted to the lips. This is a result of the ample space they require on the sensory and motor strips of the neocortex,

> "A kiss is the anatomical juxtaposition of two orbicularis orbis muscles in a state of contraction."
> —Dr. Henry Gibbons's scientific definition of a kiss (1808–1884)

and of the older *paleocircuits* (ancient brain pathways) that merge with the mammalian brain—where the feeding, grooming and emotional centres reside. As far as neurological vocabularies go, the fact that we can blow and whistle a tune testifies to our lips' fluent adaptability.

Lips also play an important role in sub-verbal language: one "bites" one's lip in vexation; "curls" one's lip in scorn; "hangs" one's lip in humiliation; is "lip deep" when being superficial; has a "stiff upper lip" when being stoic; gives "lip" or acts "lippy" with saucy talk; and pays "lip service" when proffering but not performing.

Tongue-tied for words? Like lips, tongues plunge deeply into our language: To have one's "tongue in one's cheek" is to speak with sly irony; to "hold one's tongue" is to act smart and be silent; to "speak in tongues" is to chant in religious ecstasy; and "tongue-twisters" are the all-familiar tornadoes of words that attempt to muddle our speech.

"A soft lip would tempt you to eternity of kissing."
—*Volpone*, Ben Jonson
(1573–1637)

Sonorous Delights

> *The sound of a kiss is not so loud as that of a cannon,*
> *but its echo lasts a great deal longer.*
> —The Professor at the Breakfast Table,
> Oliver Wendell Holmes (1809–1894)

Like silk whispering in a breeze, kisses are almost inaudible. How do we kiss? When we form our mouths into a "cupid's bow" we are playing a symphony of strings; a pucker is the result of a sucking movement and a contraction of the lip muscles. How empty our kisses would be without the accompanying sounds of our lips, tongues, teeth and saliva. From an onomatopoetic perspective, a kiss makes a lip-smacking noise. The very sound of the word *smack* captivates us. Indeed, it makes us smack our lips together just to say it, which is why this line by the nineteenth-century poet Robert Browning sounds so fervent: "My life did and does smack sweet." When making love, sexy sounds can signal that your partner is kissing all the right places.

According to *The Perfumed Garden* by Shaykh Nefwazi, "A kiss should be sonorous. Its sound—light and prolonged—takes its rise between the tongue and the moist edge of the palate. It is produced by a movement of the tongue in the mouth and a displacement of the saliva provoked by suction." Early sixteenth-century poet Nefwazi was writing about the kiss as a complete sensory experience, emphasizing the sound of it as much as the feel. Of course, the virtual world of the twenty-first century (where we do not necessarily have to touch in order to "connect") was far beyond Nefwazi's understanding. But the importance he placed on the role of sound in the erotic experience is far more prescient than he could have possibly imagined.

We press our lips together and emulate a sweet smacking sound into the hard moulded plastic receiver of the phone, translating sound into touch. The phone kiss jump-starts us back into our body. In the case of a dual phone kiss, two people kiss as symmetrical partners: ear to mouth, mouth to voice. The stimulation we feel, however, is a response to a concept rather than a tactile sensation. We imagine our phone kisses as they zoom through wires and air into our beloved's ear. In another sense, the phone itself "kisses" the ear of its listener. Digital signals resonate with winged kisses.

Canadian poet and futurist Christopher Dewdney explains how the telephone provides a locus for our voice in his thought-provoking book *The Secular Grail* (1993):

> The telephone is an intimate, though masked, personal telecommunications device. It is masked in the

---

Studies show that there is a significant increase in how often we laugh when we first fall in love. Furthermore, the pitch of the woman's voice is often higher at the beginning of a relationship. Giggling is often a subconscious attempt to arouse kisses.

sense that by not seeing your conversational partner you can be both intimate and impersonal at once. The theatrical nuances and capabilities of the discorporeal voice are liberated and heightened, at the same time facial and bodily expressions are invisible, focusing emotional energy on the voice alone.

The voice is a recent acquisition in terms of human evolution—a penetrating, symphonic wonder. It is in the past one million years that the pharynx lengthened to enable humans to speak. The human voice reveals not only our skills as communicators but also our background, education, character traits and emotions. "Speech is a mirror of the soul," said Publilius Syrus in the first century B.C. One can, however, have many phone personae. Voice can be intimate. Voice can be sex off the leash. And no one knows the power of the voice and tonal nuances better than phone-sex workers. They routinely modulate their voices up an octave to embrace whispery, kittenish tones and down an octave to create husky, seductive tones when soliciting a caller.

For those who are hungry to connect, the use of prosthetic communication devices (telephones, computers and cell phones) for sexual purposes not only provides places in which to explore fantasies but also offers a safe context. In addition, they lend variety to our erotic selves, temporarily interlocking us to each other in an intriguing medium of

"Her tongue with sound/doth charm my ear."
—"Her face," Arthur Gorges (1557–1625)

aural delights. Indeed, as I write, Japanese engineers are wiring cell phones to read a user's lips. (A contact sensor beside the phone's mouthpiece detects micro-electrical signals emitted by muscles around a user's mouth, and then translates them into synthesized speech or text.) Soon, perhaps, lovers will be able to mouth passionate dialogue and kisses soundlessly—and secretly—into their headsets.

"If music be the food of love, play on!" Shakespeare wrote in *Twelfth Night*, probably sensing that music could be an inspiration for tender kisses. Why is listening to romantic music so lulling? Music increases endorphin levels (the body's feel-good hormones). Newborn babies respond to music and a two-year-old is capable of composing her own songs. The right beat can induce a natural high. Euphony also affects our heartbeat, pulse rate and blood pressure. According to anaesthesiologists, music can significantly decrease the level of the stress hormone cortisol in the body. By kissing and making love to a favoured piece of music you can actually relieve symptoms of stress by decreasing the levels of this hormone while pumping up your dehydroepiandrosterone (DHEA), a hormone associated with sexual appetite. Studies have shown that music can also slow down or equalize brain waves. The slower our brain waves, the more relaxed and luxurious we feel: calm and heightened consciousness produces alpha waves of nine to fourteen cycles per second, whereas stronger emo-

> "If I were what the words are, / And love were like the tune, With double sound and single / Delight our lips would mingle, With kisses glad as birds are / That get sweet rain at noon..."
> —"An Interlude," Algernon C. Swinburne (1837–1909)

tions produce fifteen to forty cycles per second. Because the auditory nerve connects the inner ear with all the muscles in the body (vibro-acoustic memory), music improves body movement, thus reducing body tension. A slower and deeper respiration enables us to reach easier and deeper orgasms while making love. In addition, a flourish of musical notes can promote endurance, increasing performance time up to 25 percent.

The cadences of music also play a key component in dance. Dance not only synchronizes a couple's physical movements but also facilitates face-to-face contact. When undulating to music we display our emotions and physical prowess, providing our partners with an opportunity to interact with the entire body—to caress—to kiss. The actual tempo can determine the essence of the kiss. As a rule, urgent kisses embody passion, while slower kisses tend to be more romantic. Practising a little "lip dancing"—by varying kissing tempo—is the signature move of a principal smoocher. The intimate tango of lips and tongues stimulates the brain and sets into motion our oldest sense—touch.

> We are wonderfully transformed by the kiss lyrics in popular songs. In a crescendo of emotion we drink The Weaver's "Kisses Sweeter than Wine"; we steal Seal's voluptuous "Kiss from a Rose"; we fly in perpetual bliss with Faith Hill's "This Kiss." We "Kiss and Tell" (Bryan Ferry), we sigh, and then we "Kiss and Say Goodbye" (The Manhattans).

A Map of Touch

> *Kissing her fair breast, lips, cheeks, and eyes,*
> *Prov'd here on earth the joys of paradise.*
> —"Stolen Paradise," William Drummond of Hawthornden
> (1585–1649)

Why does kissing feel so good? Probably, for one, because touch is a primeval animal instinct. We all respond to touch. Our affectionate pets can verify this. Life itself could not have flourished without it. Touch is the first sense to develop in fetuses; they have been filmed sucking their own hands and stroking their umbilical cords. After birth, nursing is made possible by the guidance of the sensitive touch cells in the lips. Combine the power of touch with kissing, and what happens to your chemistry? Touch causes us to release a feast of endorphins, natural chemicals that make us glow and protect us from pain—a morphine of sorts, produced by the body. The final seduction, however, is attributed to a potent hormone called oxytocin. As it turns out, oxytocin surges just at the thought of connecting with a partner's lips. A kind of orgasmic chemical reaction occurs when we kiss, and we crave this feeling again and again. In a sense, we become chemically committed. Oxytocin and vasopressin (a hormone found naturally in the brain that is partly responsible for the formation of memories) initiate a delicious flood of desire, arousal, nipple response, erection, orgasm. Thus every kiss has the potential to chemically choreograph our carnal delights. And the sensation-hungry epidermis of our lips may explain why we want, or need, to be kissed so often.

All kisses are connected to the sense of touch, and the sense of touch is connected to the brain. When we touch our lips to someone else's our mind is reaching out.

For some people, a moustache gives the "kissee" some extra tactile pleasure. From Hollywood's early days, the moustache has signalled male virility. But attitudes toward men sporting facial hair have varied in different cultures throughout the ages. In ancient Egypt (as well as in China and India—the Sikhs of India are forbidden to remove a single hair from their bodies) the beard was regarded as the mark of high wisdom. The trend continued into the Greek civilization and endured until the fourth century B.C., when Alexander the Great commanded that his soldiers be clean-shaven. The Romans instituted the practice of the daily shave. Even so, beards and moustaches of all shapes and sizes cropped up through the centuries, keeping pace with fashion. During the eighteenth and early nineteenth centuries, the guardsman's moustache whisked to the forefront of army style, and after 1830, it became the cachet of French revolutionaries. The era of emulating film stars in moustache and manner reached a new frontier in the 1920s with

> "A kiss without a moustache is like an egg without salt."
> —Twentieth-century proverb

the arrival of a hirsute line of great lovers that began with Rudolph Valentino.

Fortunately, a person who has "lost their touch" has not permanently lost their capacity to reciprocate kisses. Medical research has long since proven what each of us knows instinctively: touching and affectionate kissing are essential for well-being. Nurses have long endorsed healing touch techniques (known as biofield therapy) to restore, energize and calm their patients' energy fields. And as the keen reader will recall, kissing is an "electric" experience: The brain's ten billion highly charged nerve cells are responsible for this electromagnetic sensation as they send pulses charging through the body's nervous system, including the skin.

Skin Hunger

O! Let me have thee whole,—all—all—be mine!
That shape, that fairness, that sweet minor zest
Of love, your kiss—those hands, those eyes divine,
That warm, white lucent, million-pleasured breast
—"I cry your mercy, pity love—aye, love!,"
John Keats (1795–1821)

Like our lips, our skin also needs to be fed. And our need for physical affection often exceeds our need for sex. Human skin is an optimal surface for touching, stroking, kissing. The biggest body organ (both by weight—2.7 to 4.5 kilograms—and surface area—approximately 1.8 square metres, or the the size of an area rug), our skin is responsible for alerting us to danger, pain, comfort and pleasure. It gives us shape. It warms us up, cools us down. Our naked skin is the premier organ of sexual charisma. The thrill of seeing a lover's skin can be extremely seductive on its own, as revealed by the nineteenth-century French poet Charles Baudelaire in "The Snake that Dances":

> I love to watch, while you are lazing,
> Your skin. It iridesces
> Like silk or satin, smoothly-glazing
> The light that it caresses.

Human skin is composed of several layers: the dermis is the lowest layer and it is mapped by blood vessels, connective tissue, nerve endings, hair follicles, and oil and sweat glands. Sweat glands secrete sweat (water, sodium chloride, urea, ammonia and uric acid) and, as most of us know, sweating can be increased when we are nervous: we often sweat over an anticipated first romantic kiss with a new partner. The epidermis of the skin (the outermost layer) consists of many layers and is renewed every fifteen to thirty days. Our skin is like an elasticized techno-fabric bodysuit complete with super-sense receptors in each hair follicle. Warmth receptors are located deep in the skin, but the tongue is one of the most heat-sensitive areas, thus making our kisses feel truly hot. Our sense of touch is even more acute on the ultra-sensitive erogenous zones of the body. Who does not respond with a delicate shiver to kisses on his neck? Or experience a swell of sensation when the curve of her hips is bejewelled by a crown of exquisite kisses. Have your beloved kiss your feet for an extraordinary sense of bliss—each foot has 72,000 nerve endings.

For most of us, caressing and kissing are essential elements during the courtship phase of a relationship. Why? The hunger for touch is an innate human need; as babies we are in almost constant skin or mouth contact with our mother's breast. Feelings of comfort, safety and love pour out when we are touched and kissed. A routine dose of contact is usually all it takes to soothe stress, elevate mood and buoy immunity. Conversely, a lack of touch, referred to as "cutaneous deprivation," can cause restlessness, depression and insomnia. For babies it can lead not only to emotional disturbances but also, in extreme cases, to death.

Breast-feeding makes oxytocin rise to such a degree that some new mothers report rippling orgasmic-like sensations. Furthermore, just touching or kissing a baby can cause oxytocin to surge, inspiring some women to want to have

---

Tactile sensitivity is not exclusive to humans. The ocean waves, quivers and vibrates with touch impulses. Giant turtles delight in the tickling sensation of having their shells rubbed. All nocturnal whiskered animals have a highly developed sense of touch or "kinesthesia" that helps them navigate through the darkness. So sensitive is our world of touch that some animals are capable of predicting earthquakes just from the static electricity pulsating in the air.

another baby to nuzzle, in order to recapture that sense of well-being. As children grow up, parental cuddling lessens, and many women find themselves suffering from an oxytocin withdrawal. The good news? Affectionate caressing and kissing can raise levels of oxytocin in both women and men. And nipples are not to be ignored: studies show that nipple stimulation (through gentle touching or kissing) is especially effective at exciting oxytocin levels in both sexes. Incidentally, men's nipples are more than just chest decorations—caressing or kissing a man's nipples and chest area can trigger a flood of feel-good oxytocin.

The connection between touch and kissing is handled differently in different cultures: In Japan, to make a move for a girl's nape is still taboo, while in Fiji, just touching a young woman's hair is forbidden. In warm, southern Mediterranean countries people are often engaged in some form of amicable physical contact. North Americans living in large cosmopolitan cities will sometimes resort to massage therapists to get their quota of touching.

The word *touch* has become a metaphor for a medley of social interactions. We are "touched" by the generosity of an acquaintance; our beloved presenting us with an armful of wildflowers is "touching." A "touchstone" is a benchmark. To possess a "soft touch" is to be generous with money; a billionaire is said to have the "Midas touch." We stay "in touch" through verbal and written messages, and we fall "out of touch" when communications cease. To add a "finishing touch" is to apply a final stroke.

Of Scents and Seduction

> *Coming to kiss her lips, (such grace I found),*
> *Meseem'd, I smelt a garden of sweet flowers.*
> —"Amoretti," Edmund Spenser (c. 1552–1599)

Of the five senses, only two are based on chemicals—smell and taste. They let us sample the elements around us for details. In evolutionary terms, smell was most likely the first sense to develop—our sense of smell pointed out what was safe to ingest.

When we kiss, a torrent of smell and taste sensations whirl through our system. Each kiss stirs our olfactory sites and carries the potential to activate powerful, sensual feelings. Our nose is always open to fresh stimulus; in fact, it flourishes on variation. Hence, every time we spritz our skin with a new fragrance we bathe our olfactory bulb (the part of our brain that processes smell) directly with impulses, because smell is the only sense that travels directly to the brain without interruption or delay. This makes smell the most flirtatious of all our senses. And the most pristine. Kiss the crown of a baby's head and take a deep breath in. What do you smell? Pure bliss. No fragrance is more hypnotic. It is one of the warmest, coziest perfumes around, and all babies secrete natural opiates (endorphins) from the moment of birth. This exceptionally kissable scent is known to calm anxieties and promote felicitous feelings.

The prominent, double-arched projection of our nose makes nose-to-nose contact inevitable when we kiss. In order to prevent a collision, we must, in fact, tilt our faces slightly before leaning in for the kiss. "Helen. In love, i'faith, to the very tip of the nose," said an attentive Paris in Shakespeare's *Troilus and Cressida*. Lovers inhale each other's kisses before their lips even touch. Then, the lips take over. A kiss is part olfactory sensation and part taste, and delightfully they mingle.

Why do we, figuratively speaking, count noses but not pairs of lips? Probably because noses are so prominent. They stick out on our faces and they demand attention. Interpreting the language of noses is not, however, as plain as the nose on your face. We pay through them. We look down them. We hold them up in the air. Instinct tells us to follow them, even at the danger of having them put out of joint. Some people have a good nose, and though still far from the trail's finish, they are usually hot on the scent.

But how do we distinguish the tens of thousands of scents that swirl rapturously around us? How does smell work?

Humans smell with a yellowish tissue located between the eyes in the roof of each nostril. This ultra-sensitive, stamp-sized patch is called the olfactory epithelium. (The patch is five times bigger in cats and therefore five times as keen.) In the epithelium, a class of cellular proteins called olfactory receptors act as the body's principal smell perceivers. It's the receptor cells that do the actual "smelling," sensing airborne concoctions. A sensational ten million receptor cells process chemical data into electrical signals that zip along olfactory nerves, delivering their signals to roughly fifty thousand cells in the olfactory bulb, just inside the cranial cavity. (Unlike any other neurons in the human body, olfactory receptor neurons are distinctive in that they can replace themselves, which they do about every thirty days.) When we indulge in a sensuous kiss, impulses are fired to the limbic area of the brain, an ancient region that governs such emotions as pleasure, desire and ecstasy. It is here that fragrance association takes place—anonymous kisses can be transmuted into the scent of a cherished smell memory.

I remember experiencing a flood of memory that was stimulated by smell a few years ago, just before I went off to Italy for a holiday. I was kissing my boyfriend goodbye when I was seized by a storm of aromatic memories. Much to my surprise, the kiss from my lover's lips invoked sweet recollections of delicious, vanilla treats of my childhood. (I later discovered that his homey scent was due to an aftershave lotion containing vanilla essence.) The association was so powerful that while I was away, I purchased a small bottle of pure vanilla extract and would twist the plastic cap off and inhale whenever I yearned for one of my amour's savoury kisses. All it took was one whiff of the earthy fragrance to be saturated by its comforting warmth.

"I have been here before, I know the grass beyond the door, / The sweet keen smell," recalls the nineteenth-century English poet Dante Gabriel Rossetti in "Sudden Light": Like a lingering kiss, smell is an enduring sense. Is it possible to re-experience amorousness simply by recalling a heady scent? Perhaps. Imagine a kiss against a backdrop of freshly cut grass, a tropical ocean breeze, a Christmas pine tree, autumn leaves—and a cascade of pleasurable feelings begins to surge inside you. Smells provide us with a remarkable amount of sensation long after the encounter. Smells can also anticipate kisses yet to come.

There is nothing, of course, like the scent of roses to set the mood for romance. The luxurious rose, with its intoxicating fragrance and hues, has seduced the senses more than any other flower. The Greek poet Sappho called it "the queen of the flowers." Roses thrill the nose every time. And the lips. Instinctively we will lift a rose to our lips and brush them with the soft, dewy petals while inhaling the heady perfume.

Cleopatra had her sails drenched with the dazzling scent of roses, fragrantly announcing her arrival at ports of call along the Nile. (An intriguing fact, considering an amazing 454 kilograms of roses are required to distill just 0.4 kilogram of rose oil, and from this a mere 0.03 percent of pure essence is produced.) In addition, she commissioned a plush carpet of rose petals, 46 centimetres deep, to help make the arrival of her Roman paramour Mark Antony more rapturous. We can only imagine the wash of kisses that flowed from this sweet-scented sea of petals.

The Romans ate, drank, gossiped and kissed while engulfed by roses. Anything said—or done—under a rose garland or chaplet (worn on the head) was *sub rosa*—a Latin expression meaning "under the rose," describing something to be kept secret. Rose petals bubbled up perfumes in Roman baths, scenting the passionate kisses that must have held thrall in these warm waters where men and women bathed together.

Pheromones

"She throws a kiss, and bids me run / In whispers sweet as roses' breath."
—*Atalanta's Race,* James Maurice Thompson (1844–1901)

The moth's kiss first!
Kiss me as if you made believe
You were not sure, this eve,
How my face, your flower, had pursed
Its petals up; so, here and there
You brush it, till I grow aware
Who wants me, and wide open I burst.
—"In a Gondola," Robert Browning (1812–1889)

Soulmates or scent-mates? A kiss encounter with Ms. or Mr. Right may just be a question of finding a partner with the "right" smell. Generally, first kisses occur when there is a feeling of chemistry. The nineteenth-century French poet Baudelaire believed that a person's libido was steered by this sensual musk. And erotic scents can linger in an already established relationship. How do we achieve this? Each of us has our own unique smell—a personal "scent signature" as distinctive as our voice, fingerprints and character. So, built into our sense of smell is the ability to sense certain chemical signals, personalized odour lures that those around us emanate, often without our being aware of them. Our skin naturally emits sexual messengers into the air. These subtle hormone-linked scents, called pheromones, are so powerful they can unleash a flood of sexual responses, such as the urge to kiss, in others.

People use pheromones (from the Greek words *pherein*, meaning "to transfer," and *hormon*, meaning "to excite") to communicate with each other. Studies reveal that they aid organisms in attracting a mate, finding food and providing protection from predators. Think of your pheromones as your personal chemical calling card. Once released, these randy secretions act as signals not only to attract but also to influence behaviour in others. But don't get sex pheromones mixed up with hormones: pheromones are the reason you feel an irresistible urge to

Since Roman times, the rose has thrived as the traditional flower of St. Valentine's Day. It is estimated that over 150 million roses—and countless kisses—are exchanged worldwide on this one day alone.

kiss a certain stranger, or what makes you compelling to a potential lover.

Since antiquity, fragrance makers have been enhancing their products by adding animal pheromones. What are the natural sources of these tantalizing aromas? Because animal-musk smells strikingly similar to human testosterone, musk is the number one kiss-worthy scent. The term *musk* is used to generically describe an entire group of odorants from various species. It gets its name from the musk deer (*Moschus moschiferus*) that inhabits the mountainous regions of the Himalayas, Burma, Tibet, Mongolia and China. Only male musk deer produce a secretion (containing musk molecules) in a pouch found under the belly. The highly seductive pheromone attracts females. Another natural musk source is produced by the civet cat (*Viverridae*) dwelling in parts of Asia and Africa. Both male and female civet cats possess glands that produce a pasty secretion that excites the other sex. A classic Islamic text, *El Ktab*, considered musk as "the noblest of perfumes and that which provokes to venery."

But humans may possess one of the most ardent olfactory aphrodisiacs around. The powerful odour in question is called androstenone, a dominant component in the gamy smell of sweat. It is partially responsible for creating a milky substance that encourages bacteria to grow, thereby converting it to a pheromonal secretion, and is associated

---

The term *pheromone* was first employed by a team of German researchers in 1959. During their studies on silkworm moths, they were able to extract an odoriferous compound that would later reveal itself to be a powerful sexual attractant. It beckoned "Come to me!" from afar. And, according to biologist Lewis Thomas in *The Lives of a Cell* (1974), a delicious frenzy of female pheromones could woo an entire population of males.

with specialized glands known as the aprocrine glands. Both men and women have aprocrine glands in their armpits, around their nipples, in their genital areas, and around their navels. Other scent-seductive support-zones include the scalp, forehead, eyelashes, cheeks and men's beards. The good news for lovers intent on kissing is that the highly potent androstenone, as well as many other odour seducers, is also found in our saliva. This means that when we are engaged in a languid kiss this scent courier diffuses naturally into our breath. The result? A bouquet of subtly perfumed kisses.

Can the "right" pheromone deepen your feelings of arousal and transform your kissing power? In a sniff. If you have ever buried your face in a lover's shirt or covered a pillow with kisses, you will have probably experienced a storm of luscious subliminal messages. Pheromones do entrance us. A baby can recognize her mother's smell even if she can't see her. Studies have shown that men can distinguish between a T-shirt that has been worn by a female or a male.

Even a woman's immunology is affected by smell. During a study on how women react to male sexual pheromones, each of the men in the study group was given a clean cotton T-shirt to wear non-stop over a weekend. The sweaty T-shirts were then sealed in plastic Ziplock bags and sent off to the lab. A group of ovulating women was asked to sniff through the stack of odorous T-shirts and rate every one for its sensory sexiness or, at least, its overall erotic intensity. Presumably an alpha male would emerge from the group—a dominant pheromonal leader of the pack. Wrong. Interestingly enough, the women subconsciously evaluated the sweat-infused T-shirts based on a group of gene codes known as the major histocompatibility complex (MHC), which are responsible for detecting diseases in the immune system. The more a man's MHC complex differed from the woman's own exclusive set, the sexier the T-shirt smell—and the man. Choosing MHC-dissimilar mates is thought to reduce the risk of genetic disease, thus producing hardier offspring. So, following your nose in choosing a sexual partner is a recipe for genetic compatibility.

The natural fragrance of a lover's body can be very intoxicating, indeed. Napoleon was said to have adored the unbathed scent of his wife, Joséphine, so much that he would write her letters from the battlefield begging her not to wash until after their joyful reunion.

The Perfume of Kisses

Where should one apply perfume?
Wherever one wants to be kissed.
—Coco (Gabrielle) Chanel (1883–1971)

The seductive power of perfume goes back thousands of years. The word *perfume* comes from the Latin *per fume* "through smoke"—celebrating the ancient use of aromatic substances, such as the burning of incense and herbs as sacrificial offerings to the gods. The early Egyptians were famous for their use of tantalizing perfumes. Both women and men of fashion swirled in waves of heady bouquet, in and après bath, from plants such as rose, lilly, peppermint and henna. They decorated their elaborately coiffed tresses with perfumed ornaments, embracing the wearer in an aura of enchanting scent. Powerful resins and unguents were also used in funerary rituals and in the embalming process, no doubt transforming the final kiss of a beloved into an enduring scent memory.

Wealthy Romans used a different scent for each part of the body. To invite kisses they would first glaze their lips with musk unguents, while aromatic spices gave their breath an erotic flavour. They poured perfume on themselves, their guests, and their pets—favourite dogs and horses were massaged with it. Exotic scents were lavishly sprinkled on floors and walls. Cascades of perfumes spilled from fountains and baths, invoking an opulent-smelling ambience for sexual escapades.

The first whiff of European perfumery began in the sixteenth century when a Roman nobleman named Flavio Orsini, Prince of Nerola, presented his second wife, Anne-

KISS AND TELL

Marie de la Trémoille-Noirmoutier, with a new perfume made with the fresh blossoms of the orange flower. The essence quickly became known as Neroli perfume and was so successful that the princess decided to scent all her gloves with it. Fragrance-dipped gloves were believed to keep the hands dewy and soft—and, therefore, more kiss-worthy. Possessing kissable hands was a top priority then, as all social encounters required a gallant hand-kiss in both greeting and parting. It wasn't long before the Neroli-perfumed gloves caught on in Europe. Suddenly everybody wanted gloves of scented leather. During the Renaissance, Italy held centre stage for perfumery, and when Catherine de Medici was to be married to the future King Henry II of France, she transported her passion for perfume with her. It was the beginning of the adventurous love affair France continues to have with fragrance.

By the mid-seventeenth century, perfumed gloves had become de rigueur in Paris. And, for the first time, a woman didn't have to be of aristocratic birth to enjoy the pleasure of having her hand kissed. In fact, anyone who could afford the scented gloves could participate in a hand-kiss rendezvous. So popular was the practice that by 1660, a guild for glove- and fragrance-makers had been established.

Scent-kisses done with virtuosity linger like the remembered cadences of a sonata. Try inhaling the breath and body of your beloved. A symphony of perfumed notes will emerge

Cleopatra was said to have rubbed her lips with pure essence before she kissed a lover, so that the captivating scent would linger long after they parted.

if you lightly nudge your nose into the intimate burrows of sex-scented flesh. All carnal odours play key roles. For example, the natural aroma of a lover's aroused genitals can act as a powerful kiss aphrodisiac. So might the armpits. Inside the elbows. Behind the knees. Around the nipples. On the throat. The breath. Which raises the question: when we kiss, where does smell end and taste begin?

To Taste Whole Joys

> *I will leave thee when . . .*
> *I have gently stolen from thy lips*
> *Their yet untasted nectar, to allay*
> *The raging of my thirst, e'en as the bee*
> *Sips the fresh honey from the*
> *opening bud.*
> —*Shakuntala*, Kalidasa, fifth century A.D.

Taste is one of our most intimate senses. And an appetizing kiss can be the beginning of a delicious journey. We can consume each other with our kisses. They are the *Babette's Feast* of the body. But what makes our romantic kisses so delectable? How does our tongue register the "sweet" sensations of a kiss? To answer these questions we must first understand how taste works. Scientists describe taste as having four qualities: sweetness, sourness, saltiness and bitterness. The word *taste* is thought to be synonymous with flavour, even though flavour is a more elaborate blend of smell (olfaction), taste (gustation) and the textural sensation of food being chewed (technically known as the "mouthfeel"). What happens when you bring a cup of creamy hot chocolate swirled with cinnamon to your lips? A rhapsody of chocolate and spice wafts up through your nose, flooding your head with aromatic bliss. The sweet, slightly bitter tastes of cocoa mixed with sugar stroke and thrill your tongue. You also experience the tactile pleasure of the liquid as it flows from your lips to your throat.

"All love is sweet," wrote Percy Bysshe Shelley (1792–1822), in *Prometheus Unbound*. Possibly. But the taste of a partner's kiss may be quite another thing. Intense reactions of rapture and repulsion are innate in all of us and can easily be evoked by sweet and bitter flavours. Perhaps the most remarkable thing about our sense of taste is our ability to differentiate between what might be hazardous to our health—such as poisonous substances—and what might be nutritionally beneficial. Scientific evidence indicates that all animals (including humans) with dietary deficiencies will consume foods that contain higher concentrations of the needed vitamins or minerals. A person with a sodium deficiency, for example, will seek out salty foods such as potato chips to boost sodium levels. An urge to ingest carbohydrates is provoked by the saccharine tastes of sugars. What is most striking, however, is the universal avoidance of bitter-tasting as well as sour or "off tasting" foods—usually an indication of their harmful toxic effects (thank goodness for the gag reflex). Sensory data from taste cells, therefore, is crucial in helping us to determine what we should and shouldn't eat. And who we should and shouldn't kiss.

Are flavourable kisses an obsession of modern times? Apparently not. In the Old Testament's *Song of Songs* (also known as the *Song of Solomon*), "Thy lips, O [my] spouse, drop [as] the honeycomb: honey and milk [are] under my tongue." The alpha males of the Renaissance pronounced their lovers' mouths as being "full of ambergris and sugar." British novelist George Eliot (1819–1880) wrote of "Kisses honeyed by oblivion" in her sensuous book *The Spanish Gypsy*.

Like literature, the tastes of language have almost always had a honeyed metaphorical flavour. We have "good taste" in partners, and often refer to our lovers as being our "sweet hearts." To be "sweet tempered" is to be amiable and act kissably kind. To possess a "sweet tooth" is to crave sugary things. And to be "sweet on" someone is to be very fond of them.

Still, there's no accounting for taste. A writer friend of mine says she has only to look at her boyfriend getting orally erotic with his food to receive jolts of pleasure.

When we chew food (or indulge in a deep kiss), chemicals called "tastants" rush through the pores of the taste buds, interact with other sensory input such as smell, and transmit a flurry of electrochemical signals to the brain.

"Watching his sensual lips savouring food excites me—I can't wait for his lips to relish me like that," she offers. The mouth-to-mouth transfer of seductive foods has long been considered a tantalizing love ploy. Taboo tidbits? In *A Midsummer Night's Dream*, Shakespeare cautions: "Eat no onions nor garlic, for we are to utter sweet breath."

What is an aphrodisiac (the term is derived from Aphrodite, the Greek goddess of love)? Generally speaking, the more exotic-looking the food, the more erotic the experience—hence the "aphrodisiac" label. And it usually implies a stimulus to kissing. "Whosoever says truffle, utters a grand word, which awakens erotic and gastronomic ideas . . ." confided Jean-Anthelme Brillat-Savarin in 1826 in *The Physiology of Taste*. Many people today use the word *aphrodisiac* to describe foods that they consider sensuous. (Casanova is reputed to have used a mélange of oysters, chocolate and champagne in some of his intimate encounters to stir up a titillating atmosphere—among his conquests were two nuns!)

A kiss can be lethal. According to recent studies, a mere brush of the lips can trigger severe reactions in a person who is allergic to what their partner has eaten prior to the kiss. The potential kiss of death can also be brought on by an allergy to certain antibiotics. How do you prevent a case of fatal attractions? Before kissing, talk about your allergies as you would talk about safe sex.

WATER OF LIFE

> *O Love, O fire!*
> *once he drew*
> *With one long kiss my*
> *whole soul thro'*
> *My lips, as sunlight*
> *drinketh dew.*
>
> —"Fatima," Alfred, Lord Tennyson (1809–1892)

Diaphanously misty kisses. Saliva rippling down hot throats like honey. Lovers' tongues dancing about the teeth and caressing each other's inner cheeks in fluid intimacy. Kisses, or the thought of them, bathe the mouth in an ecstatic wash of saliva. "Mouth, from which I sup ambrosia," wrote the Italian poet Ludovico Ariosto (1474–1533) in "Orlando Furioso":

> not ever satiated, O soft tongue, O dew;
> in which I bathe and soften my burnt heart.

From a scientific point of view, saliva is similar to genital secretions. Early Taoists believed that certain body fluids contained the life essence, and an ample exchange of these potent fluids was recommended. In the ancient Chinese

---

"I could eat you" is a well-known expression that often punctuates the kisses of hungry lovers. Though not meant to be taken literally, many a male lover in nature has been devoured by its female mate once fertilization has been accomplished. The female praying mantis and the black widow spider, for example, often seize their partners and ingest them after mating.

"Against love there is no remedy, neither a potion, nor a powder, nor song, nothing except kisses..."
—Longus of Lesbos, third century A.D.

KISS AND TELL

manual *Art of the Three Peaks*, men were advised to "drink or absorb the saliva, milk, and vaginal juices of a female sex partner." Women were similarly advised to "reap the benefits of male saliva and genital emissions." Perhaps this is what led a certain Empress Chia, who lived during the Tang Dynasty (618–906 B.C.), to nourish herself with a cornucopia of secretions collected from her court of vigorous young men.

Billions of bacteria inhabit the mouth, many on the tongue itself. (Surprisingly, clean genitals have a lower bacterial count than the oral cavity.) There are three pairs of salivary glands that trickle their secretions into the mouth. Saliva coats many micro-organisms, and swallowing washes them down to the stomach where gastric acids destroy them. The one or more litres of saliva we secrete each day helps digestion while enhancing our sense of taste. Saliva naturally contains oxygen, which keeps our mouth healthy and fresh. Everyone's saliva is unique, and is flavour-distinctive according to what one eats, smokes or even feels.

Just the anticipation of a kiss creates a kind of saliva bath, giving the teeth a natural plaque rinse. Kissing is good for our teeth. In fact, saliva actually prevents our teeth from rotting. Perhaps a deep kiss a day is all that is necessary to keep the dental hygienist away.

The author of *The Perfumed Garden*, Shaykh Nefwazi,

According to alchemical legend, the Water of Life—or dew—symbolizes the universal spirit, the secret fire, the cosmic womb. To the ancient Chinese it represented immortality; to the Druids it was the most magical of fluids.

seems to have fully understood the role of saliva and kissing. Here, an absorbing description of how to evoke a mouth-watering kiss:

> The most delightful kiss is that which is planted on moist ardent lips, and accompanied with suction of the lips and tongue, so that the emission of a sweet intoxicating saliva is produced. It is for the man to procure this emission from the woman by gently nibbling her lips and tongue till she secrets a particular saliva, sweet, exquisite, more agreeable than honey mixed with pure water, and which does not mix with her ordinary saliva. This gives the man a shivering sensation throughout his whole body, and is more intoxicating than strong wine.

Ancient alchemists considered saliva a sexual elixir. Modern scientists say that saliva contains semio-chemicals, tastes we crave when kissing our partners. So kiss and drink from the source. One caution, however, particularly in the early stages of a relationship: few lovers like to be inundated with drool. When a moderately moist kiss turns into a torrent, a second date can be a washout. Paradoxically, an over-extensive tongue tease can deplete your supply of saliva, leaving your mouth as dry as a desert. People can also get a parched mouth when the glands in the mouth that make saliva are not functioning properly, due to nervousness or lack of hydration.

Sweet Sensations

> *Sweet are the kisses, the embracements sweet*
> *When like desires and affections meet.*
> —Hero and Leander, Christopher Marlowe (1564–1593)

Ah, chocolate. The jilted crave it. The lovesick pig out on it. The premenstrual practically kill for it. What do these chocoholics all have in common? Most are searching for some melty TLC. Chocolate is said to contain high levels of phenylethylamine (PEA), a neurotransmitter in the brain that acts as a natural stimulant similar to amphetamine. It's the molecule of love. Both lust and love increase levels of PEA—studies show that PEA can also surge in response to visual stimuli such as watching a romantic movie or even day-dreaming romantic fantasies—but after a heartbreak the levels plummet. Critics, however, contend that the PEA in chocolate gets metabolized so quickly that it doesn't have very strong libidinous results. Even so, "doing chocolate" has become the jargon of many an emotional-food junkie. And some scientists say that just imagining the taste of chocolate will do the trick; the virtual sensation is enough to arouse feelings of elation. It's no wonder that the giving of luscious and love-stimulating chocolate has become a globally recognized courtship ritual.

"Chocolate is something you have an affair with," wrote Geneen Roth in *Feeding the Hungry Heart* (1982). I, for one, get quite passionate about chocolate and regularly fantasize about deep, rich cocoa interludes. My relationship with chocolate started when I was about nine—every Friday night I'd unwrap some hard squares of Baker's chocolate, carefully measure out sugar, butter, vanilla and walnuts, and pour the thick, smooth fudge mixture into a pan to set. The ritual guaranteed at least an hour of delicious foreplay: melting the chocolate and butter, stirring them until they swirled like a splendid Klimt canvas, licking everything clean, and meticulously slicing the slab of creamy fudge. My heart galloped as I lifted the first glossy square to my lips. One luscious bite was enough to send thrill sensations rippling through my body.

Carefully, we peel away the foil wrapper of one of the world's most famous chocolates. We delight in the pristine chunk tipping in our palm. It looks like a breast. Or the head of a penis. Erotically charged with delicious symbolism, we pop it into our mouth, and wait for the "kiss" to unfold. It erupts. A twirling creaminess melts delicately over our tongue. We reach the centre, a smooth marrow of hazelnut mousse. We are suddenly transported into an arena of flavour. We applaud the Perugians, the gregarious food lovers of the rolling Umbrian province. They are the *dolce*

The word *chocolate* comes from the Mayan word *xocolatl*, meaning bitter water. In 1519, the Spanish conquistador Hernan Cortéz discovered Aztecs using cocoa beans in the preparation of a spicy drink. It was thought to be the "food of gods," and the Emperor Montezuma allegedly drank fifty goblets of the chocolate beverage daily.

KISS AND TELL

vita of Italy. *Bacio* means "kiss." *Perugina* means "little Perugia." Combined they make a mouth-watering international favourite: *Bacio* or Kiss.

Conceived in the twenties, these bite-sized Kisses come in boxes illustrated with a couple locked in a romantic embrace. The entangled pair portray Franco Buitoni (founder of the famous Buitoni pasta company) and Luisa Spagnoli (a legendary fashion designer). It seems that Buitoni and Spagoli carried on a clandestine affair and decided to communicate their passion for each other via a homespun chocolate Kiss wrapped with an exclusive love message. Today the Kisses are still individually packaged in blue-starred silver foil and each *Bacio* comes supplied with an intimate message of love translated into at least four languages: Italian, English, French and Spanish.

Casanova drank a cup of chocolate for breakfast (mentioned throughout his *Memoirs*) and was an ardent believer in its seductive powers, especially where kissing was concerned. Italians from Florence soon caught on to the tantalizing tastes of chocolate and began producing their own superior lip-smacking blends. Such was the amatory reputation of the chocolate drink that monks living in seventeenth-century France were forbidden to drink it.

Chapter 5
Chemistry of Love

> *A kiss of love;*
> *The melting kiss, a kiss that doth consume.*
> —"Kissing," Edward Herbert, Lord Cherbury
> (1583–1648)

When we fall in love the world sways in ecstasy at our feet. We kiss all night. We float on air. We are love-alchemists entranced in the dance of desire.

When the sparks fly between two people, they are said to have the right chemistry. As they begin to fall in love—and kiss—an explosion of adrenaline-like neurochemicals bursts forth. In the sophisticated neuronal wiring of the brain the natural amphetamine phenylethylamine (PEA) revs up the entire system by helping impulses vault from neuron to neuron. Equally involved are the chemical cousins of amphetamines: dopamine and norepinephrine. Dopamine gives us that euphoric glow and norepinephrine is responsible for stimulating the production of energizing adrenaline. Combined, this *ménage à trois* of chemicals supplies us with chemistry. It's why our palms sweat, our knees go weak, our heart races and our stomach does somersaults. And while chemistry can cause certain undesirable physical reactions, its magic is undeniable.

The pulse of attraction begins in the largest sex organ: the brain. The human brain has an average volume of about 1,400 cubic centimetres, and weighs in at approximately 1.4 kilograms. About the size of a small melon, our brain is three times larger than the brains of our closest cousins, gorillas and chimpanzees.

The transformative software of the human brain is memory and desire. Thus, past kisses have the potential to trigger future kisses. The mere thought of one's paramour may be enough to prompt a surge of delirium. But is there really such a thing as lovesickness? The twentieth-century British poet W.H. Auden compared it to "an intolerable neural itch" in his poem "Petition." And anyone who has weathered the all-consuming storm of infatuation will recognize its signs: the heady euphoria; the lingering torment; the sleepless nights awash in a whirlwind of ecstasy—or anguish. We long for our next rendezvous. When we are

> The medieval notion of alchemy—transforming base metals into gold—was used as a metaphor by Swiss psychologist Carl Gustav Jung. He described alchemy as a method of self-transformation whereby the alchemist fuses the opposite elements within herself (that is, conscious/unconscious) and achieves wholeness. Imagine the kisses that flowed between Jung and his mistress Toni Wolf, who was not only his amanuensis but also, he believed, his spiritual muse, the *anima* to his *animus*.

with our lover we whisper silly things. We talk all night. We caress. We kiss.

And if you still doubt that lovesickness really exists, consider that in a 1992 survey of 168 diverse cultures, anthropologists discovered that 87 percent observed the traditional stages of romantic love. What's more, people have been suffering from this particular "illness" for a very long time. My favourite description of a burning pre-kiss infatuation was written in 612 B.C. by the poet Sappho on the Greek island of Lesbos:

> Your magical laughter—this I swear—
> Batters my heart—my breast astir.
> My voice when I see you suddenly near
> Refuses to come.
>
> My tongue breaks up and a delicate fire
> Runs through my flesh; I see not a thing
> With my eyes, and all that I hear
> in my ears is a hum.

From the lavish Greek culture that raised pleasure to epicurean heights to the thousands of myths, poems, books, songs, operas and legends that have followed, almost everyone knows what the fiery flush of infatuation feels like. Few sensations are as beautiful as being in love. But the brain can't maintain the blissed-out state forever. According to scientific studies, romantic love or lust endures from eighteen to thirty-six months, then, unfailingly, the dreamy spell begins to wane. Divorce rates peak around the fourth year of marriage. When the body builds up a tolerance to the chemical cocktail, it takes more and more chemistry to conjure the ecstatic quiver of passion. This may explain why some people cannot seem to maintain long-term relationships: they favour the exhilarating effects of brain-amphetamines (the new-love rush) over the tranquilizing effects of endorphins. Some people respond by becoming passion junkies. At the first signs of fading desire they're off, engaging in quick fixes with new partners. They crave, of course, that intoxicating concoction of chemistry and desire.

"What of soul was left, I wonder, when the kissing had to stop?" reflected the nineteenth-century poet Robert Browning in "A Toccata of Galuppi's." Does it have to stop? Maybe not. Neuroscientists say that a brain-chemical nasal spray capable of enhancing amorousness will soon be available.

There might be another explanation for why some relationships succeed while others fizzle. A lot may have to do with what some anthropologists call a "love map," a mental map or template that determines what excites each of us sexually—what drives us to want to kiss someone in a special way, even fall in love. I call this phenomenon the "halo

> According to psychologists, the happiest lovers engage in three types of sexual activity: sweet, tender kiss-embraces, or "comfort sex," sensational love-making sessions and "quickies."

effect." The halo effect is based on memories that we have collected since childhood in response to our parents, siblings, friends, acquaintances and experiences; we gradually develop a subliminal template for what arouses us. It could be his voice, his beard, his sense of humour, his intelligence, his warmth, his business suit, his walk and so on. By the time we reach adulthood we have formed an "angelic" image of the ideal partner, so that when we actually meet one who wears the right halo for us, it's love at first sight. In the end, a melding of compatible love maps may contribute to that warm, cozy feeling you get from being with a long-time partner.

Because romantic kisses require a certain chemistry, researchers today are concentrating on psychoneuroimmunology (PNI) to help create it. PNI is the analysis of interactions between your perception of the universe around you, the way your brain functions, your behaviour and your immune system. So that special feeling you get when you kiss deeply is not all in your head: it's gushing through your body, too. Moreover, studies have shown that passionate kissing, which requires progressive rhythmic muscular activity, stimulates alpha waves in the brain. These are the same wave-patterns that occur during periods of meditation. Since our past experiences and memories can cause us to create an ideal picture of the way we expect things to be, this, in turn, affects our mind–brain interaction, and, hence, our mind–body response. For example, when we get angry, our whole body responds by becoming tense and we react with the fight-or-flight reflex. When we are happy, such as when we are immersed in a stream of kisses, our whole body tingles with satisfaction.

Monkeying Around

> *And I would love you all the Day,*
> *Every Night would kiss and play,*
> *If with me you'd fondly stray*
> *Over the Hills and far away.*
> —*The Beggar's Opera*, John Gay (1685–1732)

According to Ray Kurzweil, author of *The Age of Spiritual Machines* (1999), futuristic technologies such as neural implants will offer a feast of sexual and emotional delights at a distance. Kurzweil maintains that chips implanted in the brain will be able to significantly enhance sensory experiences, and digitally charge us with the glow of sensuality. Think the body electric. Imagine being able to feel your lover's kisses, even when you are an ocean apart.

Kissing, caressing or coupling—mating rituals are boundlessly diverse throughout the animal world. Most of us recognize animal attraction when we see it. The customary mating position in many species has the male riding the female's back. End-to-end sex takes place in certain insects. Squid get intimate head to head. But bonobos (a kind of ape closely related to both humans and chimpanzees) are the only primates apart from humans to copulate face to face. Furthermore, bonobos possess a peace-loving, matriarchal society in which a sophisticated spectrum of sexual activities is employed to resolve differences, alleviate stress and secure social relationships.

Watching bonobos pursue each other at a zoo is like peeping at a group of sex-trade workers. The lithe, sable-furred branch of the chimpanzee family looks notably human and exhibits many of the sexual habits of people. Our last tree-dwelling ancestors gaze at each other, walk arm in arm, engage in face-to-face sex, and hug and kiss prior to coitus. They need little prompting to perform, and boast an amazing variety of sex positions. Indeed, bonobos could very well be the real Kama Sutra experts. They kiss, probing deeply with their tongues. They masturbate by rubbing their swollen genitals against each other. A female bonobo is open to sex throughout most of her cycle. And, like any modern female, she is sexually demanding. For variety she will "make love" while snuggling in her partner's lap, while in a standing position, and even while suspended from a branch. Bonobo kissing styles are equally raunchy and are always a part of foreplay. Research indicates that approximately 75 percent of bonobo sexual activity serves no reproductive purpose.

In their 1997 book *Bonobo: The Forgotten Ape*, bonobo experts Frans de Waal and Frans Lanting tell a rather amusing story about an "erotic" kiss that took place at the Wild Animal Park, near San Diego. A new zookeeper who had previously worked with a cousin of the bonobo, the chimpanzee, had quite the shock when he allowed a male bonobo to kiss him on the mouth. Rather than delivering a platonic peck, the randy ape thrust his tongue in the unsuspecting zookeeper's mouth!

In an article entitled "Bonobo dialogues" (*Natural History*, May 1997) de Waal claims that bonobos' vocal communication abilities are more highly evolved than chimpanzees. Not only do the bonobos have their own unique calls, they also convey more emotion and information about their intentions.

Anthropologists speculate that the role of "kissing" and sexual foreplay in relation to food connects bonobos to humans in their behaviour. The act of kissing, in both species, aids in sealing mutually beneficial relationships between partners. Because deep kissing is somewhat separated from reproduction, and a female is capable of coupling throughout her cycle—thanks to her strong sex drive—she can, theoretically, exchange kisses for male commitment.

Lip Synchrony

> *With arms, legs, lips close*
> *clinging to embrace,*
> *She clips me to her breast,*
> *and sucks me to her face.*
> —"The Imperfect Enjoyment," John Wilmot, Earl of Rochester (1637–1680)

You're sitting in a cafe reading a newspaper and every time you turn a page you lock eyes with an attractive stranger sitting opposite you at the next table. You nervously scratch your nose, and microseconds later he scratches his nose in exactly the same spot. You bring your hand to your mouth, and presto—he does the same. What's up? This curious behaviour is called "interactional synchrony," or "mirroring," and it is used (usually on a subconscious level) by a person wanting to impress another by copying.

The philosophy behind mirroring is one of our basic survival instincts: we are inclined to trust those who are similar to ourselves and to mistrust those whom we perceive as being different—ancient reflections, perhaps, of a clan mentality. In modern society, if you use mirroring with someone you have just met, he will instinctively know that you can be trusted, and, hence, feel an attraction to you. It is the ultimate mating dance. Mirroring is inviting because it indicates that your imitator wants to take your lead. And because you have the upper hand, it's entirely up to you where you take it from there.

When you move in perfect tempo with another—by mirroring their posture, gestures and speech patterns—barriers come down, and you sense that the person appears to be in sync with you. For instance, you're having dinner with a hot date and he's leaning forward, talking intensely about art. You can invoke a spontaneous rapport if you emulate him by leaning forward and listening intently.

How do kissing styles in the animal kingdom compare? Elephants entwine their trunks in a mutual caress. Birds "kiss" by tapping their bills. Blue whales stroke each other's flippers. Dogs like to lick. Felines nuzzle. Dolphins nudge. Green sea turtles rub heads (often migrating thousands of kilometres to breed). Male butterflies vibrate, pulsating against their partner's abdomen.

Mirroring can also be used to deflect kisses; if you lean back with one arm draped over the back of your chair, your body language will most likely signal to a would-be partner your desire to disengage or shy away from involvement. If you doubt the power of mirroring, consider the scientific fact that words account for a mere 30 percent of the message being communicated, while voice tonality and body language together account for a whopping 70 percent. What's more, your energy level, your sense of ease and your overall self-esteem—all vital prerequisites to romantic kisses—can be cloned by an attentive partner. Videotaped studies indicate that when two people are attracted to one another they will begin to mimic each other's behaviour within eight seconds.

Our mouths alone yield some telling signals that are subconsciously decoded by others. Every mirrored curvature of the lips, for example, gives us the confidence and encouragement to make our next statement in the form of a magnificent kiss. Cautious or coy? Clutch hands or madly kiss? If he's gazing deeply into your eyes, it's quite probable that there are potential kisses gathering. Darting eyes, or a fixed, unfocused stare usually indicate that the person's attention is elsewhere. When both the eyes and chin face downward, it's just a sign of shyness. Although, when the chin is pointing downward but the eyes are directed upward (recall early photographs of a demure

> "And all her face was honey to my mouth/And all her body was pasture to mine eyes."
> —"Love and Sleep," Algernon C. Swinburne

Lady Diana) it can be a charming ploy. One of the most dynamic ways a man signals that he's interested in advancing beyond cheek-kisses to the tongue-in-mouth variety is to begin to impulsively button and unbutton his jacket, or adjust the knot in his tie. The non-verbal jacket twitch can be translated: *I'm trying to be open here—help me.* Mirror the same button manoeuvres with your own jacket and you are essentially responding in kind. If your date rests his hands on his hips with his elbows projecting outward, subconsciously he is trying to make himself appear larger. This is another subtle message that spells "protection." Anyone who reaches out with her palm facing upward is signalling open-mindedness. (Palms, incidentally, make sublime kiss receptors.) A palms-up person is saying *I'm game.* Should the palm face down, however, she's letting you know that your kiss advances will most likely be spurned.

The subliminal language of legs and feet play a significant role in mating and mirroring. When someone's legs and feet are steered away from you, it's a sure signal to you to keep your distance. But, as I quickly learned while doing my field research, when a person's toes are pointed in your direction, it means he wants to socialize—the cue giving you the choice to either sidestep or meet toe to toe.

Jealousy

> *'I saw you take his kiss!' 'Tis true.'*
> *'O modesty!' 'Twas strictly kept:*
> *He thought me asleep; at least, I knew*
> *He thought I thought he thought I slept.'*
> —"The Angel in the House," Coventry Patmore (1823–1896)

"A kiss can happen suddenly without any planning or real desire to go any further," explains a twenty-five-year-old female personal trainer. After my workout, I join a group of four women in a whirlpool who are discussing their latest dating dilemmas. It seems that "Lara" has caught her relatively new boyfriend smooching another woman and has to decide whether he's guilty of sexual misconduct. Kissing, after all, may seem like an innocent gesture in itself, but Lara and her trio of friends agree that it can be a forerunner to more intimate acts. Her beau's defence, I learn, is that for true deceit to have occurred, there has to be an emotional as well as a physical component to the deed. In other words, a casual kiss does not qualify as infidelity. Lara's girlfriends all have different ideas as to how to play the game of love, but Lara firmly concludes that once you've made a commitment to someone, you shouldn't want to lock lips with anyone else. Ask yourself how you would react if you were in Lara's situation.

"Jealousy, that dragon which slays love under the pretense of keeping it alive" is the way British psychologist Havelock Ellis (1859–1939) aptly describes it in his landmark book *Studies in the Psychology of Sex*. To be jealous is to harbour a feeling of "resentment or envy on account of known or suspected rivalry especially in sexual love." In literary texts jealousy has been described, somewhat dramatically, as "a sigh of anguish," "the fear of obliteration" and "the vestige of love."

Whether the threat is real or imaginary, the painful sensation of jealousy has existed in almost everyone—at least, in anyone who has been caught in the whirlwind of love. And jealousy inspired by flirting and extracurricular kissing is as common as the flu bug. Theories about the origins of sexual jealousy abound; however, the most widespread explanation suggests that early man began to feel jealousy out of territoriality, as a natural response to protecting genetic offspring. A response to cuckoldry or desertion—or even a promiscuous kiss with a stranger—would, ultimately, help cement partners with young children to raise together.

But if jealousy is meant to be a warning signal that love's foundation needs shoring up, it is ironic that jealousy can also destroy even the most compatible relationship. Perhaps this is what Oscar Wilde was implying when he wrote in his drama *A Woman of No Importance*, "A kiss may ruin a human life."

According to the *Oxford English Dictionary*, *jealousy* is "a state of fear, suspicion, or envy caused by a real or imagined threat to one's possessive instincts."

Lara eventually concluded that a careless kiss is tantamount to cheating—it arises from a person's carnal hunger and banishes love. A month after our first discussion, in the same whirlpool, amongst the same clique of female friends, I learn that Lara and her "kissing bandit" experienced a brief reconciliation before Lara decided to let him go. Through a cloud of vapour Lara recounts her epiphany: "When we started to kiss, all I could think about was his deceitful kiss. Would our relationship soon become a docudrama of covert kisses? Realizing that I was probably wasting my time, I pressed my lips to his forehead and with one last kiss I said, 'Goodbye.'"

SEDUCTION THEORY

> *You may conquer with the sword,*
> *but you are conquered by a kiss.*
> —*Poetics*, Daniel Heinsius (1580–1655)

Seduction is at once a temptation and an invitation. Sweeter than ice-wine, a seductive kiss promises special favours. It can inspire passion as well as advance love. It can make the mind sparkle, the body glow. Seduction is an exquisite aphrodisiac because it makes you feel so marvellously desired. It is love's magic potion.

CHEMISTRY OF LOVE

We are all born to seduce. Ever since early man began to wander the Rift Valley savannahs in search of a mate, people have gone to ingenious lengths to entice the opposite sex. Why? We all have sex on the brain. According to anthropologist Helen E. Fisher in her book *The Sex Contract* (1982), kissing a female's sensitive lips could mutually stimulate partners and lead to intercourse. Moreover, arousing smooches may intensify face-to-face copulation—a boon to procreation.

Lest we think that romantic love is a relatively modern concept, for the ancient Egyptians, it was the notion of romantic love that seduced. In fact, the Egyptian hieroglyphic word for *love* meant "to desire." Pent-up passions came pouring out of anonymous love poems found written, by both women and men, in hieroglyphics on vases. In 1953, Ezra Pound translated the Egyptian love poem "Conversations in Courtship." The poem begins: "More lovely than all womanhood,/luminous, perfect . . ." The lyrics, first penned three thousand years ago, have an astonishing immediacy and a tenderness that is timeless. The writer is clearly enchanted by the object of his affection, and through the beauty of his words, the reader is equally seduced. The power of words to beguile—to seduce—is not diminished by time.

The Greeks may not have invented romantic love but

A "kissing bandit" is a term used to describe a person who has a penchant for stealing smooches with anonymous strangers. This casual approach allows kissing between individuals who will likely take things no further.

they were certainly the first to cultivate the art of seduction, when an enterprising young woman named Aspasia (c. 470–410 B.C.) arrived in Athens from Miletus in Asia Minor to lecture on rhetoric and philosophy. Her classes attracted the top philosophers of the day: Anaxagoras, Euripides, Socrates and Pericles. Pericles, it turns out, enjoyed more than her eloquent lessons: her mysterious beauty—especially her full, well-defined lips—enthralled him. She became Pericles's mistress, moved into his house, and soon after gave birth to Pericles, Junior, an illegitimate son. Irate Athenians accused her of impiety. She was defended by Pericles and acquitted. Aspasia was later credited with inciting the Peloponnesian War (431–404 B.C.).

Cleopatra's (69–30 B.C.) name has seduced imaginations for thousands of years. A woman of style, intelligence and mystery, Egypt's queen is said to have bewitched a whole line of Caesars with her exotic kisses. No great beauty, Cleopatra relied on the powerful triumvirate of fashion, jewellery and cosmetics to visually entice her august lovers. Self-possessed and voluptuous, she might have been a supermodel for *Victoria's Secret*. For Mark Antony, she was a force to be reckoned with. When Cleopatra set sail for Tarsus to meet her beloved Roman general, she went dressed as Aphrodite, the Greek goddess of sexual love. To augment the theatre, she had a coterie of boy-cupids fanning her, and clouds of rose scent that wafted to the shores. But it was, of course, Cleopatra's perfumed kisses that won Mark Antony over.

Throughout history, women have taken libidinous liberties with their lips. The kisses that the great *demimondaines* (a class of women kept by wealthy lovers—from the French *demi-monde*, or half-world, startlingly reminiscent of the Floating World of Japanese courtesans) employed to seduce their admirers are fabled. Writers Flaubert, Balzac, Zola, Proust and Colette all based major characters on these highly charismatic women with their carnal adventures. Modern art, too, is saturated with images of velvet-mouthed temptresses. They smile knowingly from canvases by such artists as Manet, Béraud, Degas, Renoir and Toulouse-Lautrec. The heroine Violetta Valéry, of Verdi's opera *La Traviata*, was modelled after Marie Duplessis (1824–1847), a dazzling seductress in real life. Greta Garbo, Marlene Dietrich, Mae West, Marilyn Monroe and Madonna all continued the legacy of the *demimondaine*, transmuting their kisses to fulfill the dreams of movie audiences.

Mata Hari (1876–1917) was the stage name of the Dutch exotic dancer and *demimondaine* Gertrud Margarete Zelle. She became a spy during the First World War and obtained information for Germany by seducing French officials with her risqué performances and her surreptitious kisses. In 1917 she was arrested and executed by the French. Mata Hari's name has since become synonymous with seduction.

> The key to seduction is building up anticipation. If you whisper in your lover's ear how you're planning to kiss him later that evening, it gives him time to let his imagination play.
>
> Gently kiss or nibble the spots that make his skin tingle, his temperature rise. Kissing the ultra-sensitive skin on the nape of his neck or murmuring sultry suggestions in his ear between light flicks of your tongue will seduce every part of him.

Whether we see it in ourselves or not, we all possess the power to seduce. "A man's kiss is his signature," said Hollywood's grand dame of seduction, Mae West (1893–1980). Men who plan on becoming great Casanovas should take time to read his eighteenth-century *Memoirs*. The Venetian-born Giovanni Giacomo Casanova (1725–1798)—adventurer, musician, traveller, writer, spy and skilled lover—categorizes autobiographically "the allurements of all forms of sensual delight " in a dizzying succession of intimacy.

We are all great Mata Haris at heart. When is the best time to stage a seduction? Vamp up your kisses on a Saturday night. Partners are generally more rested on weekends and they will have some distance from the office.

Part 2
A *Landscape of Kisses*

Chapter 6

The Art of Kissing

And there lay the lovers, lip-locked,
delirious, infinitely thirsting—
—Paulus Silentiarius (d. ca. 575)

Nothing gives us a better understanding of a culture than the way in which sexuality is portrayed in its art. The golden imagery of the Byzantine epoch, the monumental manner of the Roman reign, the passionate Baroque era, the ultra-sensuality of the Rococo period and the captivating scenes of Romanticism—all idealize the kisses of their times.

In the Graeco-Roman world, carnal iconography—featuring copulatory scenes—was widespread. Phallus worship was popular and brazen images of the male phallus (often enormously exaggerated) were engraved, painted and sculpted.

These "x-rated" representations could be found on a wide array of artifacts including everyday objects such lamps, necklaces, bracelets, bedroom walls, shop signs and so on. Why the huge fixation with phalli? They were regarded as good luck charms. Indeed, phallic amulets were worn in public places to ward off the Evil Eye; that they might be sexually stimulating was questionable.

Phalli aside, depictions of lovemaking complete with deep, mouth-to-mouth kisses were considered premium forms of artistic expression, and were likewise treated in a frank manner. (Bronze mirror-covers from Corinth, mid-fourth century B.C., were typically decorated with strikingly explicit sexual imagery of partners kissing while copulating.) Unlike contemporary pornography, which is mostly vulgar and unpliable, the erotic art of Herculaneum and Pompeii (the Roman cities that were destroyed when Mount Vesuvius erupted in A.D. 79) is profuse in ideation, humour and gender symmetry. Wall paintings of lovers from these twin libidinous towns of the first century A.D. demonstrate a delightful array of sexual positions—in which the woman is actively on top—and a banquet of delectable kisses.

Fertility was another main theme of ancient civilizations, and there were many gods and goddesses who enriched the visual arts of the times. It is through the abundantly erotic scenes in vase paintings, stone and bronze sculptures, and engraved gems that we can encounter the various deities of myth as they were recognized by the Greeks themselves.

Animals as sexual kissing partners were also depicted in early paintings. A Roman mural from Herculaneum, *Leda and the Swan*, shows a nude woman sharing a kiss with a swan while rapturously wrapping her legs around its body. A thirteenth-century illumination from a Persian manuscript of Maragha, or Maragheh, a city on the southern slopes of Mount Sahand in Iran, depicts a lion and lioness engaged in a savage copulatory kiss amongst lush foliage while exotic birds look on.

The Florentine architect, sculptor and painter Giotto (1267–1337) was credited as the first prodigy of Italian Renaissance art. He specialized in giving traditional religious themes a glowing, down-to-earth life force—a real taste of freedom after the manacles of medieval restraint. The simple yet emotionally riveting frescoes in Padua's Capella degli Scrovegni (Arena Chapel) portray scenes from the life of Christ. *Kiss of Judas* is the most ominous, featuring the forbidding figure of Judas and the winged sweep of his amber cloak as he embraces Christ against a deep-sapphire sky. The magnificent profile of the dazzlingly haloed Christ and the nefarious profile of Judas reveal a kiss of opposites. A kiss of perfect good—and of perfect evil.

The dawn of "sexual" kissing in art may very well have

> The term *Renaissance* means "rebirth" in French, and Renaissance art, which was born in Italy, generally refers to art produced in Europe from the fourteenth to the sixteenth centuries. The Renaissance saw the resurrection of the forms of classical antiquity as well as the beginning of the depiction of secular subjects.

been embraced in Giotto's fresco *Scenes from the Life of Joachim: Meeting at the Golden Gate*. Read in sequence, the murals in the Arena Chapel in Padua tell the story of the childlessness of Joachim and Anne, the mother of the Virgin Mary: how Joachim was expelled from the temple because he hadn't produced a child, and how an angel appeared to Anne with the good news that she would soon bear a child. After a sacrificial offering, an angel also appeared to Joachim announcing the upcoming birth of Mary. The series ends with *Meeting at the Golden Gate*, in which Joachim encounters his wife on his return to Jerusalem and kisses her. Mary was reportedly conceived by this kiss. What is so remarkable about this particular scene is that it portrays mouth-to-mouth "sexual activity" between a man and a woman—an activity not commonly rendered during the Middle Ages. It is likely that the *Meeting at the Golden Gate* kiss created a scandal when it was first viewed in the early fourteenth century.

One of the most seductive kisses in the world is French artist Auguste Rodin's (1840–1917) sculpture *The Kiss*. Rodin's masterpiece has also been among the most reproduced—and most forged. Rodin celebrated the human body and spirit in his art, and *The Kiss* was largely inspired by Dante's tale of Paolo and Francesca—the winsome lovers who were entwined forever in the *Inferno*. Caught in time, Rodin's naked couple are fused together in an eternal radiant

Auguste Rodin (1840–1917). *The Kiss* (detail), 1886, marble. Musée Rodin, Paris, France

kiss. Sitting on a rocky base, the woman drapes her left arm like an angel's wing around the neck of her lover. He rests his right hand on her thigh, his elegant, masculine fingers caressing her bare hip. A delicately carved nipple touches the gleaming stone-flesh surface of his chest. Muscles and veins seemingly pulse in hot, liquid ripples. Their shapely legs and arched spines pour into each other—gracefully, ravenously, the lovers kiss in a fountain of delight. The Austrian poet Rainer Maria Rilke (1875–1926) compared *The Kiss* to "a sun that rises and floods all with its light."

Immortal Embraces

> *It was thy kiss, Love, that made me immortal.*
> —Margaret Witter Fuller (1810–1850)

The worship of the deities of Greece and Rome officially ended with the fall of the Roman Empire in the fifth century A.D., yet the powerful roles of these gods and goddesses continued to be revitalized long after these civilizations vanished. During the Renaissance, for instance, many artists rediscovered the lofty immortals, and peopled their canvases (as well as works of sculpture) with representations of Aphrodite, Apollo and Dionysus (Venus, Apollo and Bacchus being their Roman names, considered more chic than their Greek counterparts). The mythological trend climaxed when virile gods and breathtaking goddesses held centre stage at the height of the Renaissance.

Correggio, whose real name was Antonio Allegri (c. 1489–1534), was an Italian High Renaissance painter. (He was named after the small town in the province of Emilia where he was born.) His skillful use of light and shadow,

THE ART OF KISSING

Corregio (c. 1489–1534). *Jupiter and Io*. 1530. Oil on canvas. 162 × 73.5 cm. Kunsthistorisches Museum, Vienna, Austria. Photo credit: Erich Lessing, Art Resource, NY

luminous colours, movement and space created a distinctive perspective. Correggio's paintings embodied religious and allegorical subjects and were characterized by sensual nude imagery. In his provocative kiss scene entitled *Jupiter and Io* (one of a four-part series depicting the loves of Jupiter, painted in 1530), the mortal nymph Io readily accepts the advances of Jupiter, who has managed to crystallize into a looming cloud with a silvery sheen. A billowing paw-like extension clasps the beautiful, naked young Io, who simply throws her head back toward us, so that we, the spectators, might better observe her orgasmic delight while receiving the tumultuous kiss. The story behind the painting is that Jupiter, a true-born playboy, took this shadowy disguise in hope of evading the detection of his wife, Juno, and seducing Io. Juno ended up catching her foggy, philandering husband in the kiss act and insisted that Io be turned into a cow. Io later resumed her original form.

In her titillating book *The Art of Arousal* (1993), author Dr. Ruth Westheimer calls it "one of the most perverse and chilling kisses in the history of art." She is describing, of course, the complex *Allegory with the Triumph of Venus* (also known as *Venus, Cupid, Folly and Time*) by the Florentine Mannerist painter Bronzino (1503–1572). He reigned as court artist to Duke Cosimo I de Medici for his entire career. His portraits influenced the tenor of European court portraiture and almost always conveyed a sense of insolent aplomb. When dealing with nude figures, such as in *Allegory with Venus and Cupid*, Bronzino paradoxically preferred to maintain what appears to have been a provocative air of critical aloofness. In the incestuous *Allegory* scene, Venus, the Roman goddess of love, is naked, except for a discarded veil, and is seated in the centre with her son,

Cupid, caressing her. His right hand fondles her excited breast; his left fervently cups her head. Venus languidly holds the golden apple she won in the beauty contest with Juno and Minerva, while teasing Cupid's curved lips with the lustrous pink velvet tip of her coquettish tongue. Meanwhile, directly behind Cupid is wizened Jealousy,

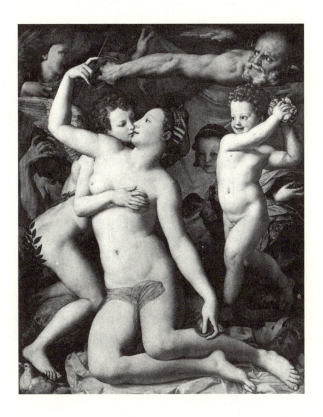

Agnolo Bronzino (1503–1572). *Venus, Cupid, Folly and Time.* (*Allegory with the Triumph of Venus*). National Gallery, London, Great Britain. Photo credit: Alinari/Art Resource, NY

tearing its hair. Fresh and youthful Folly is ready to pelt Venus with rose petals to her right. He is teamed with Pleasure, who conceals a poisonous stinger in one hand and offerings of sweet honey in the other. Above them Father Time stretches his massive arm, ready to seize the curtain and betray Covetousness—the bittersweet result of too much passion and, dare I say, too many kisses. The ivory-fleshed protagonists are posed against a backdrop of violet, rose and apple green.

The allegorical kiss was a hit. Equally erotic smooch scenes soon began to surface on artist's canvases throughout Europe. The Flemish painter Peter Paul Reubens (1577–1640) was among the artists to infuse their work with such lusty exuberance. An important Baroque painter, he was the most renowned northern European artist of his day. Reubens essentially revivified northern European painting through use of luminous colours and spirals of light that flickered across his figures unencumbered.

In his highly erotic painting *Leda and the Swan* (c. 1600–1601), Reubens reinterpreted a work that had originally started out as a tempera painting by Michelangelo. The latter master had his painting of Leda and Jupiter delivered to the French court at Fontainebleu, but, soon after, it mysteriously disappeared. Fortunately, however, several engravings had been produced; Reubens based his *Leda and the Swan* composition on one of these. The swan is none

Baroque, a movement in European painting in the seventeenth and early eighteenth centuries, was characterized by dramatic lighting and colouring, vibrant emotion, and stormy movement.

THE ART OF KISSING

Reubens (1577–1640). *Leda and the Swan.* National Gallery Collection. By kind permission of the Trustees of the National Gallery, London. Photo credit: CORBIS/London

other than the ever-imaginative Jupiter, self-transformed this time into a graceful bird in order to lure Leda, wife of the King of Sparta, into making love with him. In a warm rush of blushing tones, the swan (Jupiter) emerges from between Leda's muscular, naked thighs, curving its long phallic neck towards her mouth. Her eyes are closed while she takes his bill between her lips in an intense kiss. Notably, Jupiter's tail feathers spread forcefully against her buttocks while he engages in the passionate peck.

The Parisian-born François Boucher (1703–1770) was noted for his depictions of flushed aristocratic ladies and chubby cherubs frolicking against delicate, flower-strewn landscapes—scenes that embodied the sensuousness and the frivolity of the Rococo style. One of his most captivating paintings of a kiss was *Hercules and Omphale* (c. 1731–1734). According to the myth, even before Hercules was born, Juno's wrath and her jealousy of Alcmene (one of her husband Jupiter's infidelities and mother of Hercules) were obvious. When Hercules was ten months old, Juno tried to destroy him. The goddess let loose two huge snakes in the room where Hercules and his brother Iphicles slept in their cradles. As the snakes twined themselves around the babies, Hercules grasped one in each powerful hand, and strangled them. It was apparent that Hercules was the son of a god. But as time passed, Juno arranged to have Hercules sold as a slave to the lovely and mesmerizing Omphale, Queen of Lydia. Omphale, in turn, ordered Hercules to rid her kingdom of monsters and robbers. Admiring his heroic exploits, Omphale freed Hercules and married him.

Hercules's very name evokes the image of physical intensity. In Boucher's *Hercules and Omphale*, Omphale's scantily draped left leg is flung over Hercules's mighty thighs.

The word "Rococo" describes an artistic style of the eighteenth century. It combines the French words for *pebble* (*rocaille*) and *shell* (*coquille*) to label a mode of art born of a world saturated by sensuous objects, refined decorations, and the intimate and elegant interiors of the French court.

They both sit on a dishevelled bed that can only suggest one thing: carnal consummation. One of Hercules's massive, bronze hands firmly clasps the opalesque breast of Omphale. Provocatively displaying her neck, throat and upper-arm deltoid, Omphale kisses Hercules with passionate abandon. Cupid, meanwhile, amuses himself with a lion skin at the foot of their couch. Boucher's idyllic representation of a kiss clearly reveals a modernistic craving for an oral-erotic encounter.

Venetian sculptor Antonio Canova's (1757–1822) most celebrated sculpture, *Cupid and Psyche*, is Neoclassic in style. A European style of the late eighteenth and early nineteenth centuries, Neoclassicism is characterized by its exquisitely proportional works that resurrected the harmony and order of early Greek and Roman art. The delicious kiss of *Cupid and Psyche* is clearly a romantic gesture that has transcended time. (Images of the entwined pair are portrayed on contemporary posters as well as on countless Valentine's cards.) But, in order to truly appreciate the cool, white marble stylization of Canova's feverish figures, one must first understand the makings of the myth.

Cupid was the Roman god of love and desire, while Psyche (her name means "soul" in Greek, and was symbolized as a butterfly that escapes the body after death) was a stunningly beautiful mortal woman. Although her sisters had all landed husbands, Psyche had not one offer, due to

"I looked at nothing else in the gallery. I returned to it several times and at last I kissed the armpit of the swooning woman who stretches her long marble arms towards Love. . . . May I be forgiven. It was my first sensual kiss in a long while. It was also something more; I kissed beauty itself." So said French author Gustave Flaubert (1821–1880) of his first viewing of *Cupid and Psyche*, Canova's masterpiece.

KISS AND TELL

Antonio Canova
(1757–1822). *Cupid
and Psyche* (detail).
Marble. Photo: C. Jean

her daunting beauty. Venus, of course, was dramatically envious of Psyche's unparalleled charms, and complained to her son, Cupid. Little did she know that Cupid had already fallen captive to Psyche's beauty and grace. He would gaze at a sleeping Psyche at night and flutter unobserved from her bedside at dawn.

The solitary Psyche was lamenting her fate one day when she was carried by a soft wind to a magical palace of shimmering marble and gold. She soon became aware of Cupid's presence beside her each night: he would come and inspire her with love and passionate kisses. But when she begged to see his face, he denied her with a warning that if she were ever to set eyes upon him she would lose him forever. So they always met in darkness. Now Psyche may have accepted the terms of their recondite liaisons for quite some time had it not been for her jealous sisters. They forced her to admit that she had never even seen her lover's face and thus persuaded her to hide a lamp and light it while Cupid was sleeping. When she did so, Psyche was astonished. She did not see a monster, as her sisters had threatened, but rather a god—a splendid young god with golden curls and superbly feathered wings. Almost at once, Cupid was wakened by a drop of hot oil from the lamp that accidentally splattered onto his shoulder. Then, like an arrow, he was gone. But Cupid could not forget Psyche for long. He finally awoke her with a prick from one of his amorous spears. In time they married and had a daughter, whom they named Pleasure.

The Happy Lovers

> *The moment eternal—just that and no more—*
> *When ecstasy's utmost we clutch at the core*
> *While cheeks burn, arms open, eyes shut, and lips meet!*
> —"Now," Robert Browning (1812–1889)

It would seem that Jean-Honoré Fragonard (1732–1806), a French painter of the Rococo age, had the same vision as Browning, only his radiant lovers have managed to escape to a boudoir bathed in pastel hues to indulge in their kiss.

Fragonard was popular in the courts of Louis XV and Louis XVI for his gallant and sentimental scenes of romance, often situated in lush garden settings. His art was primarily styled on the work of the French master François Boucher. Like his mentor, Fragonard was obsessed with the theme of sensual love, and was faithful in reproducing the same quickly brushed technique of painting. Typically, his canvases were embroidered with delicate motifs of branches, frothy flowers amid washes of foliage, and fluidly posed figures (usually anonymous ladies of the court) and their lovers. Fragonard's painting *The Happy Lovers* (c. 1760–1765) reflects the frivolity, gaiety and voluptuousness of the period: a naked young woman kisses a handsome young man (still in his britches!) in a swirl of unrestrained euphoria.

To judge by Fragonard's painting *The Stolen Kiss* (1785–1790), the kiss may very well have been a planned appropriation by the young lovers. (Because of the inscription of this painting, many scholars have considered *The Stolen Kiss* to be the combined effort of Fragonard and his sister-in-law, Marguerite Gérard [1761–1837].) What we witness here is not the kind of requited kiss that one would expect of a lovely young couple about to announce their engagement. We take a more intimate look: a brilliantly satined lady proffers her cheek to her half-hidden suitor (he has been secretly waiting at the partially opened drawing-room doors for the magnificent girl to make her appearance). What does this kiss mean? Our eyes sweep diagonally across the long continuous line of the girl's extended right arm to a striped shawl that floats promiscuously from her graceful hand. And upon reaching the tip of the fabric, we finally understand what all the fuss is about: barely visible in a shadowy backroom sits a cozy group of people engaged in a game of cards. We can only assume that the girl has just raced out of that room, perhaps to get a breath of fresh air, so that she might meet her clandestine lover for a fleeting moment. Without a second to waste, they happily steal a kiss.

Abstract Passions

> *The kiss of eloquence, which doth belong*
> *Unto the tongue.*
> —"Kissing," Edward Herbert, Lord Cherbury
> (1583–1698)

Influenced by the written works of his Viennese compatriot Sigmund Freud, Gustav Klimt's (1862–1918) paintings embody the intellectual, erotic, symbolic and aesthetic passions of Vienna's dynamic *fin de siècle* intellectual world. Klimt's work is a dazzling and sophisticated synthesis of Symbolism and Art Nouveau. Characterized by the lavish ornamentation and decoration of Art Nouveau, Klimt painted large ornamental friezes of fairy-tale-like scenes, and produced evocative portraits, fusing the stylized shapes and extravagant colours of Symbolism with his own eclectic concept of beauty.

His masterpiece, *The Kiss* (1907–1908), is a glittering gala of eroticism and beauty. It shimmers sensuously like a Byzantine mosaic. A man, shrouded in heavily patterned gold, leans over and kisses a kneeling woman. Only the faces and hands of the lovers, and the flexed feet and pleasure-curled toes of the woman, are visible; all the rest is an opulent waterfall of gold, studded with alexandrites, amethysts, sapphires, rubies, opals and emeralds. A bed of petals sparkles below them.

Pablo Picasso (1881–1973)—who as a youth decided to adopt the rarer maiden name of his mother, Maria Picasso rather than get stuck with Ruiz, the more common name of his father—was probably the most celebrated artist of the twentieth century. He created thousands of works, in a thousand manners—protean series of paintings, prints,

Gustav Klimt (1862–1918). *The Kiss*. © Austrian Archives; Österreichische Galerie, Vienna/CORBIS

sculptures and ceramics—using a multitude of materials. During his artistic career, which lasted more than seven decades, he transformed art more profoundly than any other artist of his era. It might be said that he created modern art.

Three main stages characterize Picasso's erotic development, as expressed in his work. The first phase, from about 1900 to 1907, consists of watercolours and drawings inspired by the bustling brothels of Barcelona. The 1930s saw Picasso in his second phase, unleashing his sexual predator, the mythic Minotaur. In the third phase, between 1967 and 1971, Picasso's line-drawings portray a kind of cranky sexual curiosity and voyeuristic pleasure. In his 1967 group of drawings, for example, the featured couple perform a rather graphic kiss sequence (complete with hungry teeth as well as rippling lip and tongue texture) in nine engaging pieces. In contrast, Picasso's painting *The Couple* (1969) proffers a flattened perspective of two figures; the jagged contours of assorted limbs and body parts are dominated by a sunshine-yellow band of thickly painted colour, which helps to charge the childishly innocent kiss with a fresh urgency.

Man Ray (born Emmanuel Radnitsky, 1890–1976) was the quintessential leader of the avant-garde. An indefatigable experimenter, he participated in the Cubist, Dadaist and Surrealist art movements, and was a photographer, painter, collagist, object maker, printmaker, filmmaker, philosopher and poet. In 1921, American-born Man Ray relocated

Translated from French, *surrealism* literally means "over-reality." An art movement that began in France in the 1920s, it explored the unconscious mind, often using dream symbols and imagery. It confronted realism with fantasy.

THE ART OF KISSING

to Paris, where he made his living as a professional fashion photographer while in his spare time cultivating his more imaginative artistic vision. He was also responsible for creating a new photographic art—which he dubbed "Rayographs"—that involved solarized prints made by placing objects or paper cut-outs directly over photographic paper and exposing them to the light. This method gave the images an ethereal quality.

Man Ray's most famed painting, *A l'heure de l'observatoire—les amoureux* (*Observatory Time—The Lovers*; painted between 1934 and 1938), depicts an enormous pair of floating strawberry-red lips suspended in the sky. The sunny morphology of the giant mouth seems strangely appropriate in the surrounding cloudscape. The lips are just on the right side of quirky. Puffy and pulsating, they resonate beyond the

Man Ray (1890–1976). *A l'heure de l'observatoire—les amoureux* (*Observatory Time—The Lovers*), 1934–1938 © Man Ray Trust/SODRAC (Montreal) 2003

147

soft breath of the horizon, their curvilinear lines seeming to invite a kiss from the cosmos itself.

The Belgian-born painter René Magritte (1898–1967) successfully captured the spirit of Surrealistic magic. Frequently termed "Magic Realism," his works evoke a sense of secrecy and illusion. This element of mystery is best illustrated in Magritte's painting *Les amants* (*The Lovers*), painted in 1928, featuring a man and woman kissing through shrouds of fabric draped around their heads. A strangely muted blue sky lingers softly behind the couple, creating a backdrop to the baffling kiss scene. And, although it is evident they are male and female from their clothing (we are shown the top of a man's jacket, shirt and tie and the sleeveless shoulder of a woman's red dress) very little else is implied. Do they have lips? Do they have tongues? Do they know each other? What is the status of their love? Are they even lovers? The veiled forms seem to speak of a metaphysical narrative familiar only to Magritte himself. It is just as alluring, however, to ponder the sequel to their kiss.

Roy Lichtenstein (1923–1997) drew much attention to Pop painting in the 1960s with his whimsical designs of comic books and advertisements. Distinguished for his use of prominent black outlines, bold colours and patterns of dots, Lichtenstein had a gusto for parodying familiar icons in popular culture. Typically, he borrowed his imagery and style from comic books, creating exception-

---

Pop Art—an art movement that began in Britain and America in the 1950s, and that boomed in the 1960s and early 1970s—charged ahead by eliminating distinctions between fine-art and commercial-art techniques, favouring the propagation and artistic elevation of everyday objects, such as Andy Warhol's Campbell Soup cans.

ally amusing works of art that featured an undercurrent of sex as their theme.

In his 1964 oil painting *We Rose up Slowly,* Lichtenstein has placed his two Olympian swimmers in a vortex of lust. The Pop artist has depicted the desire-synchronized lovers mouth to mouth, ready to perform a submerged kiss. Or, perhaps, in après-kiss mode? The woman and man embody all the flawless characteristics of fiery comic-book fantasy: model noses, optimally curved eyebrows, perfect jawlines, luxuriant hair, astoundingly long eyelashes and full lips— all displayed in a whirlpool of graphic eroticism. The caption to the left of the painting bubbles with the illusory sentiments most likely experienced by the sex-saturated lovers following their stirring kiss.

Kiss Voyeurs

> *How often our arms slipped into new embraces.*
> *How long my kisses lingered on her sweet lips.*
> *Venus is spoiled by serving her in darkness,*
> *surely you know that sight is the path of love.*
> —Propertius (c. 54 B.C.–A.D. 2)

No other visual medium has the omnipotence to spark our imaginations like the photographic image. When viewing

KISS AND TELL

pictures of people smooching, we are like kiss voyeurs. We are drawn to engage in the lovers' kiss and to continue the pleasurable moment in our minds—to complete the action initiated by the photographer. In a sense, images of couples kissing transcend what is real in our world. They evoke an allegorical terrain where our own kiss fantasies flourish.

Embodying fresh facades of the mass-media world of glamour and theatrics, photographer Helmut Newton's work encompasses a lush spectrum of technical perfection and bourgeois decadence. Born in 1920 in Berlin, Newton is most known for capturing the sensuous contours of the naked female body. His striking photographs typically depict haute couture scenarios with stunningly beautiful models and celebrities (such as Veruschka, Paloma Picasso, Charlotte Rampling, Elsa Peretti and Jerry Hall) drenched in the decadent ultra-erotic style of luxuriant European hotel rooms and lavish gardens.

Recently, I came across an intriguing book of Newton's Polaroid shots, *Pola Woman* (1992). In it, I discovered a provocative image of two blonde Valkyries posed in a remarkably stylized kiss. The kiss seems pleasurably painted and fragrant, yet somehow elaborately staged, like a still life. The Polaroid's date reads 1974, and by the cramped angle of the models' necks and the awkward tilt of their heads, a time is suggested when two women kissing might still have evoked shock. But, of course, the kiss I want to

---

The *camera obscura*, or "dark room," first flickered into existence during the Renaissance, when it was used by Italian artists as a drawing-room aid. They discovered that light penetrating a room through a pinhole in a window shutter projected an inverted image of the world outside onto the surface of an opposite wall.

focus on and remember is the thrilling kiss of two modern lovers—their unfledged beauty, their keen lust, their lively spontaneity. Another of Newton's dauntless photographic kisses, *Le Baiser* (1982), features a crisp black-and-white close-up of a woman's assiduously painted mouth poised to kiss the chiselled bronzed lips of a man. This eye-catching pair give us only two of their features to work with: a double set of glacial mouths and imperial noses. It is, however, a masterpiece of sensual visual expression.

A poetical reportage photographer, the Parisian-born Robert Doisneau (1912–1994) liked to refer to himself as a *"pecheur d'images,"* a fisher of images. One of the world's most popular kiss photographs, Doisneau's *Le Baiser de l'Hotel de Ville* (*The Kiss by the Hotel de Ville*) appeared in 1950 in *Life* magazine. It features a high contrast photograph of a man and woman kissing on a bustling street in Paris. We are instantly enchanted. Not only does the embrace pour out profound passion and romance, it also sites Paris as the city of *l'amour*. It is no surprise that the famous kiss can be found on posters and postcards worldwide today, zealously reminding people everywhere of the preciousness of such moments of ideal happiness.

Chapter 7

Kissing by the Book

> *These violent delights have violent ends,*
> *And in their triumph die, like fire and powder,*
> *Which as they kiss consume.*
> —*Romeo and Juliet*, William Shakespeare (1564–1616)

When we're in love, we are the heroines and heroes of our own legends. We kiss under canopies of spangled skies, reliving the embraces of our favourite literary lovers. Our kisses evoke the allegorical kisses of Sita and Rama, Psyche and Cupid, Daphne and Apollo, Echo and Narcissus, Helen and Paris, Penelope and Odysseus, Aeneas and Dido, Aphrodite and Adonis, and Hero and Leander. Vibrant and wondrous, our kisses transform us into deities of desire.

In Ovid's (43 B.C.–A.D. C.18) myth of *Cupid and Psyche*,

Psyche's voluptuous kisses both delight and instruct readers: "She flung herself panting upon him, desperate with desire, and smothered him with sensual open-mouthed kisses."

The Old Testament's *Song of Songs* remains one of the most enigmatic and sensual love poems ever written. Written some time in the second half of the fifth century B.C., the text is a rhapsodic account of physical passion between a couple in the flush of spring. The sacred poem begins with the woman's voice: "Let him kiss me with the kisses of his mouth: for thy love is better than wine." In the fourth chapter (4:11) the woman's partner describes her kiss: "Thy lips, O my spouse, drop as the honeycomb: honey and milk are under thy tongue."

The soul-mingling kisses of medieval romance demanded symmetry in love and reinforced the notion of becoming one with the beloved—in life and in death. Later, literary kisses of all genres were defined with the invention, in the mid-fifteenth century, of the printing press. This meant that educated readers could spend intimate hours lingering over their favourite passages, their imaginary kisses choreographed by amorous authors. In *The Merchant of Venice*, Shakespeare's nocturnal imagery set the stage for romantic adventure:

> The moon shines bright. In such a night as this,
> When the sweet wind did gently kiss the trees.

Some books were forbidden bedmates: they provided the key to the secret garden of erotic delights where paramours lurked in every grotto.

Intimate Passages

> *Dear as remembered kisses after death,*
> *And sweet as those by hopeless fancy feigned*
> *On lips that are for others; deep as love,—*
> *Deep as first love, and wild with all regret.*
> *Oh death in life, the days that are no more!*
> —"The Princess," Alfred, Lord Tennyson (1809–1892)

German inventor and printer Johann Gutenberg (c. 1397–1468) is credited with the invention of the printing press, a method of printing that used movable type and oil-based inks, which were hand set and printed on handmade paper. His greatest publishing achievement was the *Gutenberg Bible*, printed in 1455.

The romance of Tristan and Isolde is unquestionably the most celebrated of medieval fictional love epics. This Celtic tale is believed to have had roots in the seventh century, although the legend as we know it today reached its final form in the late twelfth century. The names of the protagonists differ according to the various texts. The hero is presented as Tristan, Tristram and Tristrem; the heroine, Isolde, Iseult and Yseult. But, however you choose to pronounce it, our hero's name spells sorrow (in Italian the word *triste* means "sad"). Indeed, Tristan's name was given to him after his mother's death in childbirth. What followed was a poignant tale of passion and heartache. In brief: King Mark sends his nephew Tristan to escort the beautiful

Isolde of Ireland to Cornwall to become his queen. Isolde's mother gives a love potion to her daughter's handmaiden (intended for King Mark and his bride on their wedding night) with explicit instructions for the maid to keep it safely hidden on their journey to Cornwall. By error, Tristan and Isolde end up drinking the potion en route and fall irrevocably in love. When Tristan's uncle discovers the mistake, he banishes Tristan to Brittany, where he is promptly wedded to a second Isolde, "Isolde of the white hand." But, alas, Tristan is unable to forget his true love and becomes mortally ill. Learning that her beloved Tristan is soon to die, Isolde of Ireland hurries to him. They kiss once more—it is their last kiss. He dies as their lips part.

Out of the tempest of hedonistic lovers, Florentine poet Dante's (1265–1321) Francesca and Paolo ascend like hummingbirds in winter. Dante's epic masterpiece, *The Divine Comedy* (begun around 1307 and completed shortly before his death), is divided into three colossal volumes: the *Inferno* (*Hell*), the *Purgatorio* (*Purgatory*), and the *Paradiso* (*Paradise*). Francesca and Paolo appear in Canto V of the *Inferno*. This particular canto weaves a deep allegory around the doomed lovers concerning the theme of sin. The aristocratic Francesca of Rimini has been promised to her lover Paolo's physically deformed older brother, Gianciotto. However, this doesn't prevent Francesca and Paolo from carrying on with their clandestine encounters.

One day, while reading a book about the passion of Lancelot and Guinevere, they become so involved that they consummate their illicit love with a fiery kiss. In Francesca's words, "When we had read how the desired smile / was kissed by one who was so true a lover / this one, who never shall be parted from me / while all his body trembled, kissed my mouth." Gianciotto catches the adulterous pair and kills them in a fit of jealous rage. Their fate is known to everyone. Francesca's and Paolo's souls are sent to the second circle of Hell, where the Lustful pay for their ardour by being whipped by the violent winds of covetousness ad infinitum. But, thank heaven, there's a twist. The two lovers are "damned" in an everlasting kiss. How are we to understand this kiss? Does their never-ending affection, which survives death and endures the inferno, lighten their punishment? One has to wonder, can an immortal kiss ever be punishment?

We all become lovers when we read Shakespeare's most moving drama, *Romeo and Juliet.* The play opens at a grand masquerade ball in the magnificent Italian city of Verona. We meet Romeo and his ill-behaved friends, Benvolio and Mercutio. Later that evening, Juliet wanders out onto her balcony to imbibe some drowsy summer ambience, only to discover Romeo waiting, ready to pledge his love.

In act 1, scene V, we find Romeo holding Juliet's hand and playfully offering to kiss it. He says, "If I profane with my unworthiest hand / This holy shrine, the gentle fine is this: / My lips, two blushing pilgrims, ready stand / To smooth that rough touch with a tender kiss." Amused, Juliet joins in Romeo's caper. She responds, "For saints have hands that pilgrims' hands do touch, / And palm to palm is holy palmers' kiss." The love banter continues until Romeo finally asks for Juliet's permission to kiss her lips. When they finally kiss, Romeo expresses his delight: "Thus from my lips, by yours, my sin is purged." This provides Juliet an opportunity to cajole him into another kiss. She lets Romeo know that if her lips have taken away his sin then her lips must now bear his sin. Romeo quickly takes his sin back with another kiss. Juliet chides Romeo for kissing "by the book"—she knows he's talking a good line to get a kiss. In other words, she's in love but she's somewhat wise to men.

The eventual demise of this tragic couple is all too familiar. Desperate to reunite with Romeo, Juliet agrees to drink a sleeping potion. Romeo, seeing his Juliet in apparent death, speaks before drinking his share of the apothecary's poison:

> Eyes, look your last.
> Arms, take your last embrace, and lips, O you
> The doors of breath, seal with a righteous kiss
> A dateless bargain to engrossing death.

Juliet awakens to see her lover lying lifeless. It is too much. She takes her own life.

While researching this book I watched the Disney animated version of *Beauty and the Beast*, alongside my mother. We both established that the Beast was suitably ugly but nonetheless engaging, and that Beauty was a rare catch indeed. *La Belle et la Bête*, penned in 1757 by French writer Marie Le Prince de Beaumont as an adaptation of an original story by Gabrielle de Villeneuve, is one of the few fairy tales where the protagonists actually get to know each other before they head to the "altar." And, unlike Sleeping Beauty, who abruptly awakens to love via a single kiss, Beauty spends weeks, possibly seasons with the Beast before allowing anything libidinous to happen. Finally, in a magical moment near the end of the tale, the Beast is returned to his princely state and they both happily rejoice in the metamorphosis by way of an electric, swirling kiss. The message? True love will prevail. True love is transformative.

In 1847, Charlotte Brontë (1816–1865) introduced the world to *Jane Eyre*, one of Victorian literature's most labyrinthine tales of love. Jane, the story's heroine, is an orphan of surprisingly plain appearance who accepts employment as a governess at Thornfield Hall, a country estate owned by the stern Edward Rochester. Jane's charge is Adèle, the illegitimate child of Rochester and his deceased mistress, a French opera-dancer. Jane often hears strange noises coming from the attic, where—unknown to her—Rochester's mad wife is imprisoned, but her pride and position prevent her from asking questions. The eighteen-year-old governess gradually falls in love with her mysterious and unconventional employer. So when Mr. Rochester, who is thirty-five, asks Jane to marry him, she is overjoyed. At the wedding, however, a man interrupts the ceremony by announcing, "Mr. Rochester has a wife now living."

Devastated, Jane escapes to the countryside. She becomes a beggar until she is taken in by a certain St. John Rivers and his two devout sisters. Through the Riverses, she learns that an unheard-of uncle has died and left her his fortune. St. John urges Jane to become his wife and join him as a missionary. But Jane hears Mr. Rochester calling, an almost supernatural beckoning. Jane returns to Thornfield Hall, only to find that Mr. Rochester's insane wife has burned the house to ashes. He has been left blind and crippled by an unsuccessful attempt to save his wife's life. Desperate to find her beloved, Jane takes a path that leads to a nearby cottage. Mr. Rochester appears at the door, and in a surge of rebellious passion Jane declares:

> Reader, do you think I feared him in his blind ferocity?—if you do, you little know me. A soft hope blent with my sorrow that soon I should dare to drop a kiss on that brow of rock, and on those lips so

sternly sealed beneath it: but not yet. I would not accost him yet.

A bittersweet ending finally arrives when Jane kisses Mr. Rochester and they blend hearts forever:

> I pressed my lips to his once brilliant and now rayless eyes—I swept his hair from his brow, and kissed that too.

The enigmatic twentieth-century French writer Anaïs Nin wrote short stories, novels, journals and erotica, drawing on her intimate relationships with authors Henry Miller and Lawrence Durrell, among many others. Nin was possibly one of contemporary literature's most prolific female erotic writers. She was best known for her series of amatory journals begun in 1931, *The Diary of Anaïs Nin*. At one stage in her career she wrote "made-to-measure" erotica (due to financial pressures) that was later gathered under the title *Little Birds: Erotica by Anaïs Nin*. In her short story "Hilda and Rango" (from *Little Birds*) she takes us on a journey into the sensual world of chance meetings and anonymous kisses. One evening at a soirée in Montparnasse, Hilda, a Parisian model, falls for a swarthy Mexican painter, Rango. The lovers are soon locked in a passionate embrace: Like a rush of castanets, Rango's "hot, quick kisses" are captivating as they dance across the landscape of Hilda's body.

Like that of Hilda and Rango, the torrid affair Nin had with Miller was said to have changed her into an insatiable lover. And their love story played, no doubt, a lead role in Nin's adventurous attitude toward kissing many men.

Legendary Lovers

> *Oh, lift me from the grass!*
> *I die! I faint! I fail!*
> *Let thy love in kisses rain*
> *On my lips and eyelids pale.*
> —*Prometheus Unbound*, Percy Bysshe Shelley (1792–1822)

It is perhaps the most tragic legend of love. The romance of Abelard (1079–1142) and Heloise (1101–1164), the famed lovers of twelfth-century France, lives on primarily through their passionate letters to one another. A French philosopher, Abelard was considered one of the most important thinkers of his time. Heloise was the well-educated niece and pride of a local canon. Abelard writes in his "Historica Calamitatum":

> Her uncle's love for her was equaled only by his desire that she should have the best education which he could possibly procure for her. Of no mean beauty, she

There are many fictional lovers whose kisses continue to fuel fantasies: Sleeping Beauty and the Prince (*The Sleeping Beauty in the Woods*), Emma Bovary and Rodolphe Boulanger (*Madame Bovary*), Anna Karenina and Count Vronsky (*Anna Karenina*), Cathy and Heathcliff (*Wuthering Heights*), Ellen Olenska and Newland Archer (*The Age of Innocence*) and Lara and Yuri Zhivago (*Dr. Zhivago*).

stood out above all by reason of her abundant knowledge of letters.

Abelard was only too happy to take on the "tall and well-proportioned," seventeen-year-old Heloise—who was more than twenty years his junior—as his student. He hastily arranged to board at the canon's residence where Heloise also lived. They fell deeply in love.

> Her studies allowed us to withdraw in private, as love desired, and then with our books open before us, more words of love than of our reading passed between us, and more kissing than teaching.

Heloise's uncle discovered the careless lovers. Soon afterward, Heloise found herself pregnant. They secretly married, but Heloise was sent off to become a nun. Abelard faced a harsher punishment: he was attacked and castrated by the canon's servants. Shamed, he entered the Abbey of Saint Denis as a monk. Heloise took the veil in the convent at Argenteuil and later became a prioress. Tormented by grief over their brutal separation, the lovers communicated their devotion to each other through letters.

"First time he kissed me, he but only kiss'd / The fingers of this hand wherewith I write," reminisces the English poet Elizabeth Barrett Browning (1806–1861) in "Sonnets from the Portuguese," about her first encounter with literary soulmate Robert Browning (1812–1889). Tagged the "Immortal Lovers" by scholars, they wrote amorous lines to each other daily during their courtship. Like Heloise and Abelard, they were forced to keep their love—and kisses—under wraps, as Barrett's controlling father was opposed to the union. They too eloped. Shortly after, the Brownings departed for Pisa, Italy, and eventually settled in Florence. It was during this period that Barrett produced her most ambitious work, entitled "Aurora Leigh" (1856). The wedded lovers must have spent many passionate nights of kissing, if we are to judge from an excerpt from "Aurora Leigh" in which Barrett describes a kiss as being "as long and silent as the ecstatic night." Barrett's "How do I love thee, let me count the ways" remains among the best-known love lyrics in Victorian English poetry.

Spanish Surrealist painter and poet Salvador Dali wrote about his first kiss with his beloved Gala on the Mediterranean shore. (The dark, statuesque Gala stumbled upon Dali while vacationing at Cadaqués, an upscale seaside spot, when she was still married to poet Paul Eluard. She later married Dali and became his muse.) For Dali, this kiss symbolized "the beginning of the hunger that drove us on to devour each other down to the very last morsel."

KISS AND TELL

The Soul of the Matter

> *Soul meets soul on lover's lips.*
> —"The Indian Serenade," Percy Bysshe Shelley (1792–1822)

For centuries, writers have been obsessed with the concept of a kiss touching the soul. In "Love Palpable," the Renaissance poet Robert Herrick kissed his lover's lips and discovered "in the kisse, / Her Soule and Love were palpable"; Plato's soul "was on [his] lips as [he] was kissing Agathon"; in "Epipsychidion", Dante's rhapsodic sonnet of soulful kisses features "lips / With other eloquence than words, eclipse / The soul that burns between them"; and the early Greek poet Meleagros's soul soars with the mere thought of a voluptuous kiss:

> The wine cup is happy. It rubbed against
> warm Zenophilia's erotic mouth. Oh bliss!
> I wish she would press her lips under my lips
> and in one breathless gulp drain down my soul.

In "Le Amorose," Italian Renaissance poet Girolamo Muzio wrote of his vampiric need to "suck the live spirit from the soul of the beloved one." Aphra Behn describes a luxurious merging of souls upon the moss where "her balmy lips encountering his, / Their bodies, as their souls,

---

Here are some legendary lovers whose kisses have become icons of passion: Adam and Eve, Antony and Cleopatra, Napoleon and Joséphine, Edward VIII and Wallis Simpson, Dante Gabriel Rossetti and Elizabeth Siddal, Denys Finch Hatton and Karen Blixen, Rainer Maria Rilke and Lou Andrea-Salomé, Yves Montand and Simone Signoret, Federico Fellini and Giulietta Masina, Amedeo Modigliani and Jeanne Hébuterne.

joined," in her seventeenth-century poem "The Disappointment." The fluid kisses of Johannes Secundus bring "souls together in one breath, / Until, as the passion ebbs and begins to flow / As a single stream of life from two bodies." In "The Kiss," Dante Gabriel Rossetti's burning soul kiss is sanctified: "A god when all our life-breath met to fan / our life-blood, till love's tremulous ardors ran, / Fire within fire, desire in deity." And, instead of yearning to comingle souls, Austrian poet Rainer Maria Rilke, in "Love Song," ponders, "How could I keep my soul so that it might not touch on yours?"

In "You and I," the nineteenth-century German poet Friedrich Hebbel plunges into a hedonistic, soul-fusing embrace: "They kiss, / dissolve into one, / and go rolling into the throat's abyss."

S.W.A.K.

I will touch
My mouth unto the leaves, caressingly;
And so wilt thou.
Thus, from these lips of mine
My message will go kissingly to thine,
With more than Fancy's load of luxury,
And prove a true love letter.
—"Sonnet," J.G. Saxe (1816–1887)

A love letter is a way to pledge intimate feelings to a beloved. Mozart (1756–1791) staged a whole symphony of adoration and kisses in a letter to his wife, Clara: ". . . my love—my only one. Do catch them in the air—those 2,999 1/2 little kisses from me which are flying about, waiting for someone to snap them up." An amorous letter may also entice a lover into taking a relationship to the next level. The nineteenth-century French actress Juliette Drouet relied on flattery to arouse her lover Victor Hugo (1802–1885):

> If you knew how I long for you, how the memory of last night leaves me delirious with joy and full of desire. How I long to give myself up in ecstasy to your sweet breath and to those kisses from your lips which fill me with delight.

Not surprisingly, love letters contain passages that are the most often treasured, and the most often burned.

When kisses travelled by letter during the eighteenth century, the authors were just as concerned with presentation as with content. Masters of the epistolary package would use special parchment paper, penning quilled flourishes and kisses to their verses. The envelope was sealed with wax and secured with a silk ribbon. Among the most ardent love letters of this early Romantic period is one by Napoleon

Preprinted messages on lover's postcards appeared in Europe in the late nineteenth century and featured a flowing four-step approach to wedded bliss. The first card requested a meeting. A second card initiated romance. A third declared passionate feelings. And a fourth proposed marriage. The postcards were later replaced by the British invention of St. Valentine's Day cards.

Bonaparte to Joséphine Beauharnais, written in Paris, December 1795:

> My soul aches with sorrow, and there can be no rest for your lover.
> ... I draw from your lips, from your heart a love which consumes me with fire?
> ... You are leaving at noon. I shall see you in three hours.
> Until then, mio dolce amor, a thousand kisses.
>
> But give me none in return, for they set my blood on fire.

Shortly after Napoleon and Joséphine were wed, Napoleon left to command the French army near Italy. For months he begged her to join him in Milan to celebrate their honeymoon. Eager to embrace, Napoleon anxiously wrote in April 1796:

> But you are coming, aren't you? You are going to be here beside me, in my arms, on my breast, on my mouth?
> Take wing and come, come! A kiss on your heart, and one much lower down, much lower!

Napoleon began to hear rumours that Joséphine was being unfaithful to him in his absence. His letters—and kisses—became undeniably more passionate, as noted in this November 1796 response:

> ... You know that I will never forget the little visits, you know, the little black forest ... I kiss it a thousand times and wait impatiently for the moment I will be in it.
>
> To live within Joséphine is to live in the Elysian fields. Kisses on your mouth, your eyes, your breast, everywhere, everywhere.

Weeks passed and still no word from Joséphine. More suspicious than ever and tortured with jealousy, Napoleon penned:

> I don't love you anymore. On the contrary, I detest you. ... You don't write to me at all. You don't love your husband. You know how happy your letters make him, and you don't write him six lines of nonsense ...
>
> Soon, I hope, I will be holding you in my arms. Then I will cover you with a million hot kisses, burning like the equator.

In contrast, the letters authored by the most celebrated French literary couple of our time, Simone de Beauvoir (1908–1986) and Jean-Paul Sartre (1908–1980), offer a dis-

---

In times of war a love letter serves to nourish the heart, to keep hope alive. It is a confirmation of passion, be the contents happy or sad, nostalgic or ending with a heartfelt kiss.

How does one write a spellbinding love letter? Start by using a pet name that only you and your lover share. Describe your most potent kiss desires—detail all the places on your body where you'd like his lips to linger. Amatory letters, like kisses, can be left unfinished—and thus stir the imagination.

arming, frank dialogue. Through the letters, we get a rich glimpse of their love life. In their fifty years of uninterrupted correspondence, the intellectual lovers always used the formal *"vous"* and addressed each other with the same affectionate endearment—*"mon tout petit"* and *"cher petit vous autre."* Anyone who loves to read wartime letters will be captured by the French lovers' tender, epistolary, goodnight kisses.

It's no surprise that epistolary romance has gone electronic. But the question is, can intimacy be ignited on e-mail? There is a riveting moment in Leo Tolstoy's nineteenth-century novel *Anna Karenina*, when Levin writes a proposal of marriage to Kitty while she watches him pen the words. What separates writing something down by hand from whisking off an electronic message is that the former upholds a gesture of commitment—it is an act of courage. With letters, you're venturing into unknown territory because you don't know what the other person is thinking. An ideal love letter is one where the respondent reads the lines and simultaneously hears, in the mind, the writer's voice, the way we hear a voice-over to convey the reading of intimate letters in film.

Suzanne Boyd, editor-in-chief of *Flare* magazine, articulates the nuances of penning belles-lettres: "I like writing love letters: sometimes spoken words are just not enough. When something is put on paper it makes it more of a keepsake. Love letters are cherished for a lifetime."

"A love letter should be like kissing your beloved with words," says Boyd. "The right words can enhance a sensuous element, like a soundtrack adds to a film. So, if you really want a person to remember a special moment—or a spectacular kiss—you might describe it in glorious detail."

Chapter 8

Cinematic Kisses

> *Shall we go learn to kiss, to kiss?*
> *Never heart could ever miss*
> *Comfort, where true meaning is.*
> —"A Report Song," Nicholas Breton (1542–1626)

Tender, romantic, flirtatious or erotic, a kiss is often the climactic moment of truth in a film. Whether it signifies love at first sight, forbidden love, unrequited love, obsessive love, first love, spiritual love or tragic love, on-screen kissing is the culmination of passion, and sometimes the surrogate for sex. What made film kisses so stimulating in the old days was that consummation was left to crystallize in the spectator's imagination.

A film kiss is mute yet intensely articulate. Music can

heighten the emotion of an almost-silent screen kiss—throaty orchestral sounds drench the airwaves and get our own lips thirsting. Though the kiss involves only a momentary fusion of lips, time slows down as we identify with the actors. And everyone, it seems, learns how to kiss from the movies. Through the visual aid of moving pictures, inexperienced lovers can dramatically improve their technique.

The first screen kiss was recorded by the Edison Company in a brief 1896 production called *The May Irwin–John C. Rice Kiss*, or, simply, *The Kiss*. Inspired by a scene from the hit Broadway comedy *The Widow Jones*, *The Kiss* consists wholly of a man and a woman caught in the act of smooching. (Rice repeatedly breaks away to stroke his monumental moustache as the celluloid flickers on.) But what had been acceptable on stage was considered unsuitable for the cinema. The thirty-second close-up was deemed erotica by the public. One scandalized Chicago publisher, Herbert S. Stone, wrote: "The spectacle of their prolonged pasturing on each other's lips was hard to bear ... Such things call for police interference." Of arrests, there were none.

Ironically, the silent films of the 1920s featured some of the most tantalizing kiss scenes in movie history. The smoky-eyed Theda Bara (1890–1955) held centre stage as the first "vamp"—so called because of her "vampirish," or sexually aggressive, approach. In *A Fool There Was* (1915), Bara seduces a married diplomat, turns his career upside down, then leaves him in financial ruin. When it appears that things are finally getting back to normal in his life, Bara returns and demands a kiss. He succumbs to her request—and becomes her ill-fated lover. Bara's "man-eater" kisses continued to feed the imagination of audiences in such movies as *Sin* (1915), *Cleopatra* (1917), *An Unchastened Woman* (1925) and *Madame Mystery* (1926).

But just when the reels began rocketing, the fiery portrayals of sex (and violence) managed to inflame America's moral guardians. In 1934, a code of ethics created by the Motion Picture Producers and Distributors of America, under William H. Hays, embraced a strict set of guidelines that would govern film content for the next two decades. The Hays Code set forth a somber do's-and-don'ts list concerning what could and could not be shown in American movies. Specific regulations regarding sex and kissing scenes were paramount:

> ... The sanctity of the institution of marriage and the home shall be upheld. Pictures shall not infer that low forms of sex relationships are the accepted or common thing.... Scenes of passion should not be introduced when not essential to the plot.... Excessive and lust-

John Barrymore (1882–1942) delivered the most kisses in a single film—127 in the movie *Don Juan* (1927). Leading ladies Mary Astor and Estelle Taylor played the saturated recipients.

ful kissing, lustful embracing, suggestive postures and gestures, are not to be shown.

Seduction or rape should be never more than suggested . . . They are never the subject for comedy.

Under the code, the "treatment of bedrooms must be governed by good taste and delicacy." Beds were twins and always featured a pair of prominent reading lamps. And even married couples were forbidden to lie together on a bed—one of the pair had to keep a foot on the floor during a kiss scene.

Nonetheless, in 1939, two spectacular kisses managed to emerge from one film: *Gone with the Wind*. Based on the romantic 1936 novel by Margaret Mitchell, this Civil War epic tells the story of Scarlett O'Hara (Vivien Leigh) and Rhett Butler (Clark Gable), one of fiction's most tempestuous couples. The first kiss in the film to send sparks flying takes place on the road to Atlanta, when Rhett tries to embrace the reluctant Scarlett in a farewell kiss. Cunningly, he tells Scarlett that he wants to "carry the memory of (her) kisses" with him into battle and that she need not worry about how much she loves him—it's the kiss that matters. It is an unforgettable scene set against a blazing, fiery-orange landscape. When Scarlett doesn't respond, Rhett ruggedly forces the kiss. Much later in their story, Rhett, now Scarlett's husband, comes home drunk

Mae West and Anna May Wong were the only film divas never to lock lips with their leading men.

and, once again, forcibly kisses her. As powerful as this scene is on the page, the film's creators masterfully capture Mitchell's erotic, descriptive prose on screen. Although she resists at first, his passion sweeps her away with an irresistible force. When she finally reciprocates, their ardent kiss thrills both of them with excitement and joy. The moment of Vivien Leigh's next-morning smile remains one of the most graphically suggestive in film history.

In 1966, U.S. Supreme Court decisions concerning profanity brought a dramatic revision in the Hays Code. With the new code, kiss scenes of any length could be shown, providing they didn't contain explicit acts of violence. By the late 1960s, films were classified by a rating system according to their suitability for viewing by young people.

20th-Century Foxes

Her kisses
Dissolve us in pleasure, and soft repose.
—"Damon and Cupid," John Gay (1685–1732)

Improvising or not, one thing is certain: They don't make kisses like they used to. Nowadays, filmmakers generally skip the romantic foreplay and get straight down to R-rated business. In fact, most of Hollywood's most memorable kisses are found in films of classic vintage. Take Lauren Bacall and Humphrey Bogart in *To Have and Have Not* (1945). Bacall in the character of Slim initiates what will be her first kiss in her first film with Bogart (playing Steve) in one of the screen's most famous seductions. The scene opens with Slim nuzzling into her new boyfriend Steve's lap and surprising him with a flirty kiss. He asks her what she meant by "that" and she coyly responds that she'd been "wondering whether [she'd] like it." A true appraisal of his kissing expertise requires a second peck. After kissing him again, Slim stands and heads for the door. Midway, she propositions him with the well-known line: "You know how to whistle, don't you, Steve?" After she has left, Steve gives a wolf whistle, and then, still seated in his chair and smoking a cigarette, he chuckles to himself. The tough-guy hero is clearly stunned by the bewitching Bacall, who didn't think twice about taking the first-kiss initiative.

Another undeniable vixen of the twentieth-century screen was Ingrid Bergman; her sexy catch in Alfred Hitchcock's *Notorious* (1946) was Cary Grant. This suspense classic revolves around Alicia (Bergman), the daughter of a convicted Nazi spy who is asked by the American government to penetrate a lethal German cartel by going undercover. Assigned to accompany her on her mission is the deadly handsome intelligence agent Devlin (Grant). We can all guess what happens next. Hollywood's sexiest screen idols pair up for one of the most extended film kisses ever—three minutes. The "notorious" kiss scene begins on a balcony and is interrupted when the phone rings. They nibble and kiss each other on the ears, nose and lips as they traverse the room to answer the telephone. The staccato kissing continues throughout the phone conversation—Hitchcock's ingenious way of eluding the Hollywood censors. (The Hays Code wouldn't allow any smooch over three seconds long!) It is an ephemeral triangle among Bergman, Grant and the viewer. We are reeled into this intimate kiss sequence with breathtaking anticipation, even if it is altogether tame by today's standards.

During the 1950s, romantic kissing was considered an acceptable sexual act. And the prospect of seeing Elizabeth Taylor and Montgomery Clift (in their prime) doing *anything* together at a black-tie gala is reason enough to revisit the 1951 classic *A Place in the Sun.* In this tale of doomed romance, based on a novel by Theodore Dreiser, director George Stevens zoomed in so close on the young lovers' faces that they look like amorous titans. (For years after this film was released, just about every teenaged girl in the U.S. modelled a pair of Liz's glimmery pearl-drop earrings at her high school prom.) Clift plays a poor boy from the wrong side of the tracks who is smitten by ravishing rich-girl Taylor. The celebrated kiss takes place on yet another balcony—amidst the high-society swirl and schmooze of Taylor's high-class crowd. The tender kiss replays in Clift's mind, as well as on the screen, in the film's heartbreaking final scene.

Clad in nothing but swimsuits, Sergeant Warden (Burt Lancaster) and Karen Holmes (Deborah Kerr) find forbidden passion in the Hawaiian surf in *From Here to Eternity* (1953). The adulterous lovers meet for a secret rendezvous on a secluded moonlit beach to engage in one of Hollywood's most dynamic kiss scenes. The movie was based on author James Jones's smouldering 850-page, 1951 novel of the same name, borrowing its title from a Rudyard Kipling poem called "Gentlemen Rankers": "damned from here to eternity." Although the author set the famous kiss in a hotel room—with an ocean view—director Fred Zinnemann took it one step further. By placing the lovers on the edge of the fathomless ocean, he tapped into a powerful symbolism of all that is deep, wild, unpredictable—and erotic. As the foamy waves crash over Lancaster and Kerr's intermingling bodies, their brine-drenched kiss represents orgasm. When later asked what it was like filming the memorable beach scene, Lancaster responded, "It was cold, and I was wet!"

Strangeloves

> *Though I with strange desire*
> *To kiss those rosy lips am set on fire.*
> —"Kisses Desired," William Drummond of Hawthornden,
> (1585–1649)

A sort of cousin to Dr. Strangelove, *Harold and Maude* (1971) shows that passion has no age barrier. This cult film made by Hal Ashby (Colin Higgins wrote the screenplay) stars one of cinema's oddest couples: a wealthy twenty-year-old (Bud Court as Harold) with a death wish, and a spirited octogenarian (Ruth Gordon as Maude) who simply teems with joie de vivre. Obsessed with exiting this world, Harold transforms his new sports car to look like a mini-hearse, spooks his blind dates, and attends funerals, at one of which he encounters the eccentric, high-on-life Maude. Unconventional to the bone (nude modelling is one of her many avant-garde pursuits), Maude teaches Harold the pleasures of life and how to make the most of his time on this planet. And when he caresses her, the sixty-year gap between them is unquestionably trestled: Maude demurely tells him that he makes her "feel like a schoolgirl again." On her eightieth birthday, Harold decides to propose to Maude, and when he gives her a meaningful kiss on her lips and then embraces her in a slow waltz, they become like any infatuated couple. But just when Harold is about to present her with the ring, we discover that Maude has taken a fatal dose of pills that will cause her death in a few hours. Uplifting Cat Stevens melodies surge in the background as the two lovers kiss and declare their undying passion for each other. We reach a sublime finale: Maude's last words to her young beau are "Keep on loving."

"Love has no age, it is always new-born," wrote the seventeenth-century French genius Pascal. And so it is in Giuseppe Tornatore's *Cinema Paradiso* (1989). This inspiring film tells the story of a boy, Salvatore (played, as he ages, by Salvatore Cascio, Marco Leonardi and Jacques Perrin), in a southern Italian village after the Second World War. Salvatore forms a friendship with aging projectionist Alfredo (Philippe Noiret), and falls in love with the movies. Their only obstacle is the local priest, Father Adelfio (Leopoldo Trieste), who pre-screens Alfredo's films and has him cut out all the kiss scenes. (Not unlike the Hays Code in Hollywood.) Disregarding his promise to return the "censored" cuts (in this case kisses) to the distributor, Alfredo keeps the spliced negatives and puts them together in a montage, which he bequeaths to Salvatore. In the film's finale Salvatore finally gets to see all the smooches that had been sequestered from the films of his childhood. His face lights up with a smile full of both longing and longing fulfilled.

KISS AND TELL

In *Cyrano de Bergerac* (1990), based on the play by Edmond Rostand (1868–1918), French director Jean-Paul Rappeneau has us thrilling at Cyrano's lusty swordplay one minute and deeply touched by his gallant wordplay the next. Gérard Depardieu stars as the eponymous hero, the seventeenth-century lovelorn poet and swordsman who articulates his love for his cousin, the beauteous Roxanne (Anne Brochet), by proxy, through the Baron Christian de Neuvillette (Vincent Perez), a drop-dead hunky soldier she loves. Cyrano is anguished by the belief that his extra-large nose will prevent him from ever finding true love.

When Roxanne confides her love for the gorgeous but tongue-tied soldier, Cyrano agrees to narrate a romantic tête-à-tête on Christian's behalf. The balcony scene remains the most celebrated moment in *Cyrano de Bergerac*. As planned, Christian takes position one stormy night under Roxanne's balcony and repeats the phrases that Cyrano whispers to him from his hiding place in the bushes. Christian's maladroit delivery of Cyrano's lines, however, soon prompts Cyrano to take over. He imitates Christian's voice and, still under the dark cover of bushes, shapes his desire in dazzling poetic imagery. Roxanne responds by declaring her love. Beside himself with intoxication, Christian bolts back in and asks for a kiss. Cyrano does some serious damage control when he hastily adds, "How

> "A kiss is a secret told to the mouth instead of to the ear."
> —*Cyrano de Bergerac*, Edmond Rostand

shall we define a kiss?" and then soars into author Edmond Rostand's eloquent definition. A kiss is:

> A promissory note . . .
> . . . on the bank of love.
> The "O" of love on waiting lips.
> A secret with the mouth as its ear.
> Eternity in the instant
> the bee sips.
> A flower-scented host.
> A way to know the other's heart
> and touch the portals . . .
> . . . of his soul!

Cyrano successfully seduces Roxanne by proxy but, because of the success of their escapade, loses her in marriage to Christian. Nevertheless, all ends happily in this tragicomedy when Cyrano and Roxanne (who is by now a widow) share an endearing kiss, between pillars of moonlight—in spite of his overshadowing nose.

KISS AND TELL

Deeply Bonded

> *But his kiss was so sweet, and so closely he pressed,*
> *That I languished and pined till I granted the rest.*
> —*The Beggar's Opera*, John Gay (1685–1732)

I have always had a thing about Florence. The ecstatic landscape. Lush sun-kissed hills, and their soft, blue-green slopes that enfold the city on three sides. The Arno River languidly flowing westward to the plain. The ancient towers. The stone flourishes of the Renaissance facades. And the expressive Florentines who live everything in the moment, passionately, fleetingly.

Adapted from the novel by E.M. Forster (1879–1970), the film *A Room with a View* (1985) opens in Florence in 1907. A young woman, Lucy Honeychurch (Helena Bonham Carter), is visiting the city with her older cousin and chaperone, Charlotte (Maggie Smith). They stay at the charming Pensione Bertolini, but are unfortunately booked in a north room without a view. Before they even get a chance to properly vent their concerns, a certain Mr. Emerson (Denholm Elliott) insists that the women take his quarters, which offer a south panorama of the Arno River and the famed Ponte Vecchio, topped by Vasari's corridor of shops. (The impressive bridge was built between 1345 and 1564, and features three segmented medieval-style arches on massive

---

Some two hundred years ago, the French writer Stendhal was reported to have been so enraptured by the beauty of Florence that he actually became ill. Even today, tourists to the city have been known to be struck by "Stendhal's Syndrome" (severe light-headedness due to an excess of beauty), making a trip to the nearest *pronto soccorso*—hospital emergency—a necessity!

piers, with arches above.) Lucy gets an even more breathtaking view of life when she makes the acquaintanceship of Mr. Emerson's handsome and free-spirited son, George (Julian Sands). One day, while on a sojourn in the hills, George takes the opportunity to kiss her amidst a waving sea of barley and fiery-tongued poppies. Their kiss is astonishingly naked, echoing the perfection of blossoming spring. Lucy's cousin Charlotte witnesses the ardent embrace and decides they must return to England immediately.

Back home in Surrey, Lucy resumes her rapport with Cecil (Daniel Day-Lewis), a tiresome bibliophile to whom she is engaged. Thank goodness George re-emerges and befriends her younger brother, Freddy (Rupert Graves). (There is a thoroughly delightful scene of the two young men and a priest skinny-dipping and frolicking naked in the forest.) Lucy tries her best to ignore George's advances, but he finally corrals her and kisses her again. Lucy must now choose. Does she submit to a cerebral but certainly passionless life with Cecil, or does she allow her feelings for George to run wild? She chooses George, naturally.

They marry and somehow manage to float away to Florence to spend their honeymoon at the same pension where they met. We catch their silhouettes in a kiss and embrace by the open window. Cathedral bells can be heard echoing their opulent noon chorus, while the antique city glitters gloriously in the background.

"The well-known world had broken up, and there emerged Florence, a magic city where people thought and did the most extraordinary things."
—*A Room with a View* (1908), E.M. Forster

KISS AND TELL

In today's salacious cinema, a kiss on the mouth is par for the course, but *Pretty Woman* (1990) turns that assumption on its ear and makes kissing a forbidden, and therefore newly erotic, act. Edward Lewis (Richard Gere) is a millionaire corporate raider who takes a wrong turn and ends up on Hollywood Boulevard, where he meets a vivacious prostitute, Vivian Ward (Julia Roberts). She steers him back to his Beverly Hills hotel and charms him into hiring her for the rest of the week. But first they must settle the contract terms. Vivian opens the negotiation by asking Edward what he wants sexually. He wants a synopsis of what she will do. "Everything," she responds, but she doesn't kiss on the mouth. Kissing "gets too personal" for Vivian—she never lets sentimentality get in the way of her work. That settled, Vivian is handed $3,000 to stay and is sent on a Rodeo Drive fantasy shopping spree. The hooker with a heart of gold soon melts Edward's heart, and he wins her adoration. Together they lounge, watch old films, bathe, dine, go to the opera, and spend luxuriant hours reading in the park. So when Vivian finally kisses Edward, the moment is extraordinary. She walks out of the bathroom wearing expensive lingerie and silently approaches Edward, who, in his blissed-out state, has fallen asleep in bed. She leans over to kiss him, ever so tenderly, and accidentally wakes him up. Lots of sweet kisses follow until the two lovers are passionately entwined.

The following day, Vivian's prostitute friend asks her if she has kissed Edward on the mouth. When the answer is "yes," we know for sure it's love. Vivian gets the full fairy tale when at the end of the film her silver-haired Wall Street knight sweeps up to her flat in a white stretch-limo clutching a bunch of red roses. What could be more romantic?

In *The English Patient* (1996), a brush-stroked cave painting of a swimmer swirls us onto the wavy contours of the Tunisian desert. Based on the novel by Michael Ondaatje (the film adaptation was written and directed by Anthony Minghella), the story is set during the Second World War, and concerns Count Almásy (Ralph Fiennes), who is found horribly burned, by Bedouins in the desert. Assumed to be English, he ends up being cared for in the ruins of an old monastery in Italy by nurse Hana (Juliette Binoche), in the wake of the Allied advance. Slowly, his story of a fervent love affair with a colleague's wife, Katharine (Kristin Scott Thomas), begins to appear through a series of poignant flashbacks. The poetic and evocative puzzle is pieced together gradually through the dying patient's worn, leather-bound pocketbook of the *Herodotus*, which includes photographs, notes and drawings that he has written and pasted inside, and that Hana is asked to read aloud.

KISS AND TELL

There are three kisses, in the film, of great effect. The first is what I call the "kiss of the plum," a "kiss" of nourishment that takes place between Hana and her declining patient. Hana has just discovered plums in the orchard. She peels a plum and exuberantly slips the sweet flesh between his lips. His mouth moves slowly with the ecstasy of the taste, some juice trickling from the corners. The English patient is touched by the sensual "plumness" of the fruit.

The second kiss scene takes place in Almásy's room in Cairo. He is seen napping, fully clothed, on his bed. A fan whirrs overhead. There's a knock at the door. Then another. A third. It's Katharine. She walks into the room, a luminous figure in a cotton frock, afternoon sunlight pouring an aura around her. Almásy rises from the bed and goes to his lover, kneels before her, buries his face in the folds of her dress. Distraught at having been separated from her beloved, Katharine begins to slap Almásy on his face and shoulders. Then her fingers cradle his head. She dusts some sand from his hair. He pulls back, gazes at her. She kneels down and they cover each other with violent kisses. Hungry kisses. Desert kisses. In a moment of blind passion, Almásy grabs hold of her dress and tears it from her body.

Near the end of the film, Hana is at the English patient's bedside in the monastery. She picks up a hypodermic and a phial from a nest of morphine ampoules, to prepare his injection. Almásy reaches out and pushes a lethal dose towards her. He nods with his eyes and faintly whispers, "Thank you." His mind drifts back into the sheer sepias of the desert. He swims toward his beloved's cold body in the cave. Hana bends down and tenderly kisses him on the mouth. This third kiss signifies supreme maternal love.

Not unlike the "endless" kiss sequence in Hitchcock's *Notorious*, the original *The Thomas Crown Affair* (1968) contains a scene where the camera makes a 360-degree psychedelic orbit around self-made millionaire-turned-bank-robber Thomas Crown (Steve McQueen) and his insurance-investigating nemesis Vicky Anderson (Faye Dunaway), as they smooch and "revolutionize" their relationship.

Actors Pierce Brosnan and Rene Russo replace McQueen and Dunaway in the 1999 remake of this film, directed by John McTiernan. The second version of *The Thomas Crown Affair* focuses on the romantic adventures between Crown, the dashing playboy thief, and the hot-on-his-trail investigator Catherine Banning. His latest crime: stealing a $100,000,000 painting from what appears to be the Metropolitan Museum of Art in New York. It is no surprise that he is a kleptomaniac, though when it comes to beautiful women, he is even more adroit at stealing kisses. (Brosnan, after all, is the current James Bond.) He's also the kind of guy who bets $100,000 on a single golf stroke. The story ends with an especially soaring kiss. Banning is seen crying in her solitary plane seat when a man's hand, holding a white handkerchief, appears like magic from behind her. "Did you set this up?" she screams hysterically to her bemused lover. Not waiting for a response, she flings herself over the seat (with amazing agility!) into his lap and attacks him with an intensely voluptuous kiss. An exquisite close-up of Russo's perfectly lined, apricot-glazed lips fills the screen. The chemistry between the actors is breathtaking.

CHICK FLICKS

Kiss me again, and kiss me still, and kiss.
Kiss me again, your kisses are like wine.
Kiss me again, seal me and countersign,
And I will give you this — and this — and this —
—"Sonnet XVII," Louise Labé (c. 1520–c. 1566)

Foreign cinema has always been a hotbed of ideas. Sexual ones. Girl-meets-girl ones. German-born Marlene Dietrich got things rolling by becoming the first Hollywood leading lady to kiss another woman, in 1930, in *Morocco*. Dressed in a tux and donning a top hat she crisply smacks the lips of a stunning woman. Dietrich went on to play many provocative roles in Hollywood's *film noir*.

In German director and screenwriter Max Färberböck's *Aimée & Jaguar* (1999), a passionate love affair (based on a true story) begins between two women living in Berlin in

1943, amidst the bombing raids and the daily threat of genocide. Until the war, the delicately beautiful Lilly Wust (Juliane Köhler) has led a conventional life: She is a good housewife and an über-mom of four children, to boot. Her husband, Günther (Detlev Buck), is a good-looking soldier on active duty. The couple have a relationship that is somewhat conventional, but by no means uninhibited—both have had their share of brief encounters. But when Lilly meets a young and charismatic woman at a concert one night, her life dramatically changes. Initially, Lilly is unaware that Felice Schragenheim (Maria Schrader) is Jewish and living in the underground, and that she is in constant danger of being arrested by the Gestapo. Like a magnet she is pulled toward this playful and clever creature who mysteriously disappears for days on end without a rational explanation. Lilly instinctively feels that she is the object of Felice's desires, and she wakes up to her own lesbian yearnings one afternoon when Felice embraces her and plants a kiss on her mouth. Lilly has never experienced such a potent kiss before. Bewildered, she slaps Felice and abruptly turns away. It is Lilly's mouth, however, that betrays her; we witness an exquisite, irrepressible inner smile that lets us know that something important has begun, something from which she will not be able to escape. They make up names for each other, Aimée (Lilly) and Jaguar (Felice), used as nicknames in their love letters, which they feverishly

> The French term *film noir*, or "black film"—coined by two French film critics in 1946—refers to the dark mood and high contrast black-and-white lighting of an American film genre that was largely modelled on the Expressionist film techniques and lighting used by German directors in the 1920s and on the French poetic realism of the 1930s.

write to each other every day. Eventually Lilly divorces her husband, Felice moves into her flat, and the two lovers make a pact of marriage.

Kissing Jessica Stein (2002, directed by Charles Herman-Wurmfeld and co-scripted by stars Jennifer Westfeldt and Heather Juergensen) takes a contemporary look at the subject of romance and the single woman. When we first meet Jessica (Westfeldt)—a twenty-eight-year-old New York journalist—she is emotionally spent. Her best friend is pregnant, her brother is engaged, and she hasn't met a decent man in a year.

After a dating spree from hell, an intriguing personal ad is brought to Jessica's attention by a co-worker. Jessica thinks that the person in the ad sounds ideal for her—the only snag is that the ad is in the "woman seeking woman" section. Still, on an impulse, she answers it and meets Helen Cooper (Juergensen), a quirky art gallery director. They meet for drinks and, to Jessica's surprise, they "connect." Their evening of banter climaxes in a kiss when Jessica and Helen are walking together on a downtown sidewalk. Jessica has just stated that she knows how she would react to anything when Helen suddenly plants a slow, meaningful kiss on her lips. Jessica is left standing dazed. But when we see her the following day at work, she is glowing.

Their next rendezvous takes place at Helen's loft. Seated side by side on a sofa, Jessica and Helen have a discussion about lesbianism. Not wanting to appear clumsy on the subject Jessica blurts out that she is going to have to "go slow." But each time Helen moves in for a kiss, Jessica interrupts with a question, such as whether they should use their tongues. Scenes of the two lovers smooching ensue, with Jessica commenting that each subsequent kiss was their best ever.

Kissing Jessica Stein, ultimately, is about female bonding. When the two women decide to live together, their sexual relationship is anchored by their kisses—here, the intimate outcome of their friendship.

Chapter 9

Lipstick: Elixir of Seduction

> How she would smother me with kisses, and, oh,
> ye gods, what luscious ones they were!
> —*The Love Books of Ovid,* Ovid (43 B.C.–A.D c. 18)

Lipstick has the power to tantalize, to transform, to transfix. It is the S.O.S. of makeup, the international code of desire. It commands attention. Authority. Attendance. It transcends other cosmetics in its ability to remain moist and supple on its wearer's lips despite the fact that this enigmatic feature is almost always in motion. (The only other oral feature to rival a plush set of lips is the glossy tip of the tongue. Both are wet and shapely, both are used when kissing—characteristics that make them alarmingly provocative.) A painted mouth sets the mood and provides valuable insight into its proprietress's intentions, such as the kisses to come. The feeling—indeed the taste—of a kiss is quite different with lipstick, as lipstick contains special emollients that lubricate lips. Like the ancient alchemist's transmutation of common metals into gold, lipstick is the contemporary elixir of seduction.

Lipstick is the number one quick-fix cosmetic purchase—it tops the toiletry "most essential" list in response to the if-you-could-bring-one-thing-to-a-desert-island-what-would-it-be question. Not surprisingly, lipstick is also the most commonly shoplifted cosmetic.

Why do females enjoy painting their lips? For many young girls, the act of applying lipstick is a coming-of-age ritual—a rite of passage from girlhood to womanhood. By smearing her lips with her mother's candy-apple-red the child seems to cry out, *Now I have womanly power*. Didn't it work for Lolita? Later on, lipstick provides a spellbinding formula—a relatively inexpensive way to recast yourself. In *A History of Make-up* (1970), author Maggie Angeloglou aptly states that lipstick symbolizes "adventure, glamour, and high living at a low price." My mother's tropical-pink creation from Max Factor in the 1970s seemed to suggest anything was possible.

Fashionable Egyptians in ancient times would enhance their puckering appeal by staining their lips with iron-oxide-tinted clay. Archaeologists have found five-thousand-year-old samples of lip rouge and other cosmetic formulas,

The word *elixir* is one of the most magical words in alchemy. Its meaning ranges from "quintessence" to "vital spirit" to "potion of eternal love."

some of which contained such lethal ingredients as lead and mercury. These toxic substances most likely succeeded in going straight into the bloodstream of the wearer. (Perhaps such lip colour produced the first kisses of death?) That Nefertiti, Queen of Egypt, set out to face the afterlife with a stockpile of cosmetics, we can be certain. Cleopatra swore by rich carmine-coloured lip stains made from the crushed carapaces of red beetles. Even Roman men got in on the action by wearing lip colour to the battlefield, to appear more vital and threatening to their enemies.

The Italian Renaissance celebrated its own standard of idyllic lips. In 1548, Firenzuola, an Italian monk and man of letters, published *Dialogo delle Bellezze delle Donne* (*Dialogue on the Beauty of Women*), in which he states "the mouth was to be small with medium lips, vermilion in colour and not to show more than five or six teeth—uppers only—when parted." Elizabethan women tantalized and seduced with lips smudged with geraniums and crushed roses. But by the late seventeenth century the British put the lid back on rouge pots by passing a law declaring makeup a form of witchcraft used to entice a man into matrimony. (Quite the opposite message of today's aggressively made-up supermodels, some as young as twelve, that can be found pouting suggestively in an array of publications.) Inhibited Victorians would steal some colour by secretly kissing rosy-pink crepe paper. The less bashful bathed their lips with brandy to make them appear redder and more kissable. In the early nineteenth century Chinese women were blossoming into pink glows. Using carmine, they blushed not only their cheeks and lips but also the tips of their tongues and nostrils. The whole face was a rippling landscape of arousing delight.

Now, this love affair with ruby lips has had some rough patches. A countess's beauty manual, published in the early 1900s, maintained, "the lips should be a pretty red strawberry colour, but the colour should be achieved through health, not cosmetics." Another noble-minded authority on holistic lip colour, the Baroness d'Orchamps, suggested in *Tous les Secrets de la Femme* (1907), "Soak the lips for at least five minutes in a glass of warm water. Dry them, then smear them with camphorated pomade. After a quarter of an hour, dry them again with a soft cloth and put on some glycerine. Unless you are seriously anemic, your lips will become as red as carmine . . . A light sucking of the lips, a little bite, will give to them in an instant a crimson bloom." In 1915, the wholesome Gibson Girl, an idealized American image of beauty, was discovered biting her lips and sucking on hot cinnamon drops to acquire a redder and more swollen effect.

Modern women can't seem to get enough of the artificial pucker appeal. Pop culture has given us a myriad of colours to suit every mood. The palette has widened to include everything from deep crimsons to clovery mauves to full pinks to golden mochas to silvery nudes. New textures that give lips the butterscotch glossiness of glazed doughnuts have revolutionized our kissability. Mattes, cremes, sheers and shimmers complicate making a choice at cluttered cosmetic counters. But the invention of long-lasting formulas that can survive sips of champagne, or a luscious kiss, is the real innovation of lipstick technology.

Lipstick advertisements only add to our confusion: they conjure an illusory mode of gratification. I decide to consult with a professional makeup artist. She tells me that any colour can look deceiving when camouflaged in its protective cartridge, so testing its actual hue, to see how it works with skin tone, is crucial. For starters: the bigger the mouth the better. To add *oomph* I am told to fill in the entire shape of my mouth, going a fraction beyond the natural outer lip line. In fact, a too-scrupulous application of bold colour will only diminish an otherwise naturally pert mouth.

To make sure I don't have lipstick on my teeth, I'm instructed to purse my lips (after its application) as though I were about to kiss actor Antonio Banderas, insert my index finger into my mouth, then slowly pull it out. Any lingering colour ends up on my finger. I am reminded of the traditional Kleenex method of tissue-kisses that my mother, and most of the women of Paramount Pictures, used to employ. In 1928, when Kleenex was invented, one could whisk off a coupon to get a free sampler of the new cleansing tissue.

Gentle and disposable, the Kleenex handkerchief grew into a domestic necessity—one very significant use being as a blotter for lipstick, as women quickly discovered.

THE KISSING MACHINE

> *Eternity was in our lips and eyes,*
> *Bliss in our brows bent.*
> —*Antony and Cleopatra*, William Shakespeare (1564–1616)

July 1982. My best girlfriend and I deplane in L.A. and we are greeted by the city's three goddesses: sun, heat and glamour. We head to the Max Factor Museum (now the Hollywood History Museum) on Highland Avenue, just a jog south of Hollywood Boulevard. The museum is like a polished Art Deco jewel, glittering amidst the grey urban sprawl. Huge terra-cotta pots of windy palms lick cinnabar tongues of sunlight on the marble facade. We are both reminded of the romance of Hollywood. In a flush of emotion, we kiss each other's cheeks.

Max Factor's specialty was to transform average-looking people into dazzling stars. Back in the 1930s and 1940s, the world of movie makeup was dominated by this aspiring young immigrant from Russia. It all started when movie comics turned to Max Factor, searching for a new makeup that wouldn't melt under hot lights. (He introduced cosmetics to the public in the 1920s, with the promise that every woman could look like a movie star by using his products.) The result was greasepaint in a tube. Soon after, he invented Pan-Cake, false eyelashes and lip gloss. The movies took on a new charisma with such stars as Jean Harlow, Claudette Colbert, Bette Davis, Rita Hayworth, Ginger Rogers and Judy Garland all flaunting Max Factor–enhanced features. Even the water-resistant, ruby-red lipstick colour worn by Ester Williams in her swimming scenes for MGM, during the 1940s and 1950s, was a Max Factor innovation. The waterproof cosmetics were originally created for Rex Ingram's silent film *Mare Nostrum*, in 1925. Supposedly, the stirring underwater scenes could not be completed without such makeup. The Technicolor version of the enduring formula was so successful that it has since been used lavishly on the lips of hundreds of movie stars ever since.

Following our tour guide, my friend and I learn that the original Max Factor studio contained four celebrity makeup rooms, each one labelled by hair colour and decorated to bring out the best of a star's complexion: "For Brownettes Only" was done up in flattering shades of soft peach; "For Brunettes Only," dusty pink; "For Blondes Only," powdery blue; "For Red-heads Only," in pale mossy green. Beauty heaven, we think.

As we continue our trek though the museum we are mesmerized by a curious device called The Kissing Machine.

Created in 1939, the enigmatic black box, reminiscent of a surreal adding machine (Man Ray comes to mind), features two sets of his and her rubber lips that when pressed together, under ten pounds of pressure (2.25 kilograms from him and 2.25 kilograms from her), tests the indelibility of lipstick. The lips were modelled on the mouths of a young couple, engaged to be married, who were plucked from the Max Factor production department. The twosome, in their naïveté, volunteered to test the new lipstick creation, but after months of paying lip service, they tired. (All the facial muscles are used during a passionate kiss and we burn about 6.5 calories a minute when we kiss amorously.) That's when the machine came in. With bright lipstick smeared on her pair of simulated lips and a tissue placed midway between the two mouths, a super long-lasting lipstick named Tru-Color was born. Lucille Ball, from television's *I Love Lucy* show, was the first Hollywood actress to test-drive the colourfast formula. Apparently even "Ricky's" steamy Latino kisses, in the Tropicana nightclub scenes, wouldn't rub it off.

Red: Colour of Passion

> *Your sweet lips are not lips, but coral, soft and red,*
> *That binds our every sense with bonds of crimson thread.*
> —"To His Mistress," Jan Andrzej Morsztyn (1621–1693)

It's the shade of glamour, strength, power and passion. Femmes fatales have flaunted it. Geishas have served tea and erotic fantasies wearing it. Cate Blanchett reigned as Elizabeth in it. Paloma Picasso is never seen without it. It means serious business: red lipstick. I never go to an art opening, reception, gala, fashion event, or even my book publisher's boardroom without my signature lipstick colour—a magnificent peony red that advertises my sexual pluck. Or so I like to believe. Considered a lethal part of a woman's kissing arsenal, a cardinal lip stain aims at firing up the most sensual part of the face. *Read my lips*, it warns. *Listen to my desires*, it urges—even if I haven't uttered a word. In their exquisite, pas-de-deux storm of sunset colours, carmine lips shout, *I know what to do with this mouth!* Georgia O'Keeffe's (1887–1986) highly erotic painting *Red Canna* comes to mind—an intimate flower vagina that ripples open in an impulsive wave of delectable pinks, bronzy cocoas and lustrous fiery-reds. *Kiss these glorious lips*, it flashes.

Our everyday world proffers a visual avalanche of reds—all the reds that spill out as fruits, wines, spices, flowers,

---

Red is a powerful colour. It can excite, alarm, seduce, charge up. Studies show that just seeing the colour red has been known to increase our metabolic rate by 13.4 percent. It also improves blood circulation, and spurs on the production of red blood cells.

autumn foliage, birds, tropical sea creatures, sunsets, minerals, rooftops, fire engines, sports cars, neon signs and even red carpets. Red stimulates the brain; it hits our senses like a hornet's sting. This is probably why red is associated with courage, determination, assertiveness, sensuality. Red lips want to conquer. They follow through. They demand centre stage. It's no wonder that Marilyn Monroe, Bette Davis, Lucille Ball and Madonna all chose red.

Portrait painters of the late eighteenth century, notably Gainsborough, were connoisseurs of the bright red mouth. Back then, a chalk-white face ablaze with magenta cheeks and cadmium-scarlet lips, as witnessed in Gainsborough's leading-lady portraits, was all the rage. Red mouths were viewed as an invitation. An article in *The Gentleman's Magazine*, written in 1792, stated: "If the young men of this age are so silly as to be allured by a little red paint, why red paint must be used." Today, supermodels sporting ruby pouts, in bold contrast to an almost deathly pallor, project a preternatural knowingness from catwalks in Milan, Paris, London and New York.

Not only does red have a powerful sexual connotation, it also has a certain kiss-and-tell quality that cannot, and should not, be overlooked. Although an appliquéd set of red lips on a man's collar could be a woman's way of being remembered or even adored, it usually signals the desire to leave a personal signature behind—to mark your sexual

"I cease not from desire till my desire
Is satisfied; or let my mouth attain / My love's red mouth, or let my soul expire,
Sighed from those lips that sought her lips in vain..."

—"Diwan," Hafiz
(1320–1391)

territory. In both film and life, red kiss impressions have acted as accomplices to crimes, helped to dissolve marriages and provoked many a sumptuous fantasy. Indeed, red lipstick always manages to leave its mark, whether on cheeks, clothing, wineglasses, sheets, mirrors—or, most importantly, on the mind.

WANDS OF HERMES

You have witchcraft in your lips, Kate.
—*Henry V*, William Shakespeare (1564–1616)

A swish of crackling plastic and sliding metal—I expertly twist the slender rod out of its sheath and give it a quick glance. The lipstick is pristine, untouched and lustrous. I guide it toward my anxious mouth, lips parted. The moist wand glissades easily over them. I press the sticky surfaces together into a perfect kiss. Suddenly my mouth radiates flashes of fuchsia and gold. There are few things sexier than opening up a new lipstick and testing its effects. It is pure ecstasy. And the ceremony of touching a phallic-shaped tube to the lips, in a slow, spellbinding kiss, could not be lost on any lover. This purse-size magical baton is the ultimate feminine weapon.

The first American-made metal-slide tubes of lipstick appeared in 1915. Commanding the most attention in the early 1930s was the well-chiselled Lancôme lipstick case dubbed *Clef de Coquette* (Coquette's Key). When opened, the receptacle's phallic overtones were undeniably present. The sculpted gold-toned casing with its pulsating head of red was marked by symmetry and Hollywood glitz. Its use seemed to contain the power to transform any mouth into a star's mouth; women who used it, the product promised, would suddenly find themselves lounging in *The Blue Angel* (1930), their seductive Dietrichesque lips prompting kiss scenes. There is a remarkable similarity between the stylized *Clef de Coquette* case and the sophisticated facade of American architect Philip Johnson's "Lipstick Building" in New York City (at Fifty-Third Street and Third Avenue), built in the mid-1980s. In his biography of the American architect, *Philip Johnson: Life and Work* (1994), author Franz Schulze explains that the Lipstick Building was so nicknamed "on account of its elliptical plan and the two setbacks in its elevation, which endowed its shaft with the look of a giant retractable lipstick tube." Compact or colossal, lipstick's packaging is always tantalizingly sexual, almost graphically so.

Emerging from lustrous sheaths, lipsticks come in three basic shapes today: the wedge (rounded tip, one side angled); the teardrop (pointed tip, one side angled); and the fishtail (both sides angled). And like any in-the-palm-of-the-hand phallus du jour, a lipstick must have a certain weightiness to be taken seriously. When clasped between two fingers, a tube should be heavy enough to convey its powerful alchemy yet light enough to make a hasty disappearance into an evening bag.

No matter its size or shape, every tube of lipstick comes loaded with its own retractable tongue. Thrusting up, it is like the smooth, blunt snout of a porpoise rising mischievously out of the waves. The warm, waxy wedge of lipstick is deliciously reminiscent of the tongue, that bundle of fibres, nerves and taste buds that savours, licks, swallows, extends and explores in a deep kiss. And, in our mouths, responding rapidly to the slightest stimulation, are the tiny egg-shaped Meissner's corpuscles that lie between the epidermis and the dermis. These oral sensation receptors specialize, as do other hypersensitive erogenous zones—the fingertips, nipples, clitoris, penis, tongue and lips—and are especially responsive when something, such as lipstick gliding across our lips, touches them. What woman can resist the lush sensation of such dewy silkiness caressing her lips? What man is not titillated watching a voluptuous hot-pink wand kiss the parted lips of his lover?

Immaculate Mouths

> *For a glance: the world;*
> *For a smile: the heavens;*
> *For a kiss . . . I don't know*
> *What I'd give for a kiss!*
> —"For a Glance," Gustavo Adolfo Bécquer (1836–1870)

Backstage at a Gucci show, live mannequins sit shivering in their G-strings while a jet-set clique of hair stylists and makeup artists forms a nimbus around them. Tacked to the wall is a sketch of a model's head, her features embellished by a carnival of colour. One of the artists picks up a lip pencil and begins to apply dots along a model's upper lip line and dashes along the bottom of her lower lip. He then connects the dots and dashes. He looks up and studies the sketch briefly, then, using a fine lip brush, he carefully fills in the lips with an electric apricot colour. To redefine her mouth shape, and to stop the lipstick from "bleeding," he goes over the boundary of her lips again with the pencil. A dollop of sheer gloss completes the exquisite mouth-*de-mode*. A *whoosh* of nectar gushes out in spasms, like a flurry of ocelots. A set of burnished lips, thick as golden butterscotch, follow. Next, a mouthful of orchids comes to life. A procession of luxurious Tuscan lips circle in the amphitheatrical light. Drinking in the photographers' flashes, the models' mouths are the most ultra-erotic accessory on the catwalk. And after pouring out their last pirouette of vibrant lip hues, the models change back into their jeans and steal on homeward, some with their elaborate mouths still painted, glimmering in the Milanese night.

Lips come in a variety of natural shapes and hues. One's lips can be narrow or thick. Bulge out or sweep in. They are capable of pouting, frowning, smiling, pursing. A tiny or "dainty" mouth, for example, was considered most alluring in Victorian times. The "rosebud" mouth was a fashionable lip style in the 1920s. Clara Bow, the leading lady of silent film, had pert lips shaped like a bow. Puckered "vampire lips" were also big in the silent film era, often transforming kisses of passion into kisses of death. Garbo's were sculpted thin. Joan Crawford sported a canoe-shaped pair that were given the title "bee-stung." The early 1950s saw Ava Gardner posing as one of the popular Vargas "pin-up" girls with shapely lacquered lips. Marilyn Monroe flashed a star set of voluptuous lips in *The Seven Year Itch* (1955). And, of course, Julia Roberts hypnotized us all with an extraordinary painted smile that filled half her face in *Pretty Woman* (1990). Today, Angelina Jolie sports the ideal pair of lips, big and fleshy like sugared fruit gums. Kissability, however, remains in the eye of the beholder.

Lip liners appeared in the 1990s, giving everyone a chance to make their lips seem more abundant. More kissable.

> "A man had given all other bliss, / And all his worldly work for this, / To waste his whole heart in one kiss, / Upon her perfect lips."
> —"Sir Lancelot and Queen Guinevere," Alfred, Lord Tennyson (1809–1892)

Pushing the larger-than-life mouth at the end of the century was RuPaul, New York's inimitable gender illusionist who served as a spokesperson for M.A.C. lipstick—primarily a bright siren-red colour called Viva Glam.

I remember being invited to M.A.C. headquarters in Toronto to do an interview with Frank Toskan, one of the cosmetic empire's founders. It was a blustery March day. After climbing a steep flight of industrial stairs, I entered a room of slick hydraulic-black surfaces. Sinking into a soft leather chair, I gazed around. I couldn't help but notice some lipsticks on a desk that conjured up images of bullets. Cooing over me was a poster of RuPaul. She was dressed to seduce in a slippery, cherry-red, skin-tight PVC bodysuit and matching platform boots. But it was her ready-for-sex parted lips that dominated—*I am the "It" girl*, they growled. Every muscle of her taut body seemed to converge at her lips. The first real "trophy" mouth.

Nowadays anyone can own a pair of lavish lips with the help of collagen implants—or a professional's touch. A Canadian fashion designer friend, Tu Ly, demystifies the much sought-after lip transformation without collagen in an exclusive, step-by-step account of a photo shoot he did in London with Germany's über-model Claudia Schiffer.

"She stepped out of a limousine wearing an army surplus jacket, cable-knit sweater and faded denims, hauling an over-sized, celery-green leather tote. Her famous blonde hair and large, dark sunglasses suggested the universal do-not-disturb sign reserved for celebrities. In Puma's, she darted through the courtyard and into the photo studio. As soon as she was in the makeup chair I got to witness her trademark high cheekbones, remarkably piercing blue eyes and wide pale lips. Her unadorned skin glowed. A splash of freckles gave her a look of innocence. But what struck me most was her mouth: how the corners seductively curved up."

After a brief consultation with the team's makeup guru the transformation began: "We started by arranging the famous tresses onto large cylindrical rollers. Next we pruned her eyebrows to fine-arched perfection. Little *maquillage* was required on the delicate complexion of the Nordic icon—a dab here, a dab there. Forty minutes flew by. At last, the celebrated mouth. The already impossibly pouty lips were first outlined in soft raspberry. A rich plum lip colour added texture; every stroke of the lip brush made her lips seem fuller and more fruit-like. Then the rollers were removed. With a quick shake of a head, locks tumble into bouncy waves. She has suddenly metamorphosed into a seductress. Teetering on sky-high stilettos, she steps in front of the camera. The soft spin of a fan blows her into dreamlike slow motion. The supermodel throws sharp, bankable *Vogue* poses with an amazing ease—each move wielding hypnotic gazes and outrageously kissable lips. She

"You are always new. The last of your kisses was ever the sweetest..."
—John Keats (1795–1821), in a letter to Fanny Brawne

mesmerized everyone on the set." With every outfit change, the makeup artist further manipulated Claudia's mouth, varying lip colour from demure pink to flaming red. Each new transformation celebrated a new fantasy persona. "She morphed into the contemporary heroine that I personally adore. First sweet, then tough—a quintessential chameleon." Had the Bardot of our times finally shed her innocent image in a single brush of the lips? Eight hours later, Claudia was scrubbed back to her original fresh self and dressed in her street garb. The enigmatic blonde planted fashionable yet memorable kisses on my friend's cheeks before zooming off. "I was completely enamoured. Of course, that's the spell of lipstick—with the right colour and application, you can be anything."

Captivating, cajoling, capricious and bursting with carnality—lips are eternal bastions of optimism. Fuelled by kisses, they can make a lover's body shiver and the erogenous zones warm and electric. Returned kisses allow us to experience an in-the-moment, planet-stopping rapture. Our kisses flow from season to season—an endless saga of life, mystery, miracle and love.

This is how we kiss.

Epilogue

Encounter Redux

A kiss can tell us everything about love. All relationships begin with a kiss and romantic kisses stir within us. Kisses rise in shivers of yearning, like a secret charge that needs to leap out. Like summer lightening. Kisses dance, they wriggle, they slip away.

The power of a kiss is revealed to us through our senses. From the glow of her skin to the flavour of his mouth, the alchemy of a kiss goes far beyond our ephemeral dreams. For most of us, the perfect kiss is physically and emotionally mutual, the lips of our beloved more delicious than we could ever imagine.

Lips have their own eros and we have all tasted the nectar of passion. I can still remember the many kisses I exchanged with my beloved while living in Venice years ago. Life stood still on wine-tinted evenings and romantic repose. Our kisses were as exotic and wondrous as the winged lion statue that presides over St. Mark's Square.

Now it is winter, an ocean and a continent away and icicles, hot from the breath of window panes, gleam in the moonlight. Inside the cosy room we kiss, our lips enchanting landscapes. How they found us, this blizzard of kisses, I will never know. But to help encourage us to keep kissing there is Robert Herrick (1591–1674), one of the most celebrated masters of eternal kisses, in his poem "To Anthea: Ah, My Anthea!":

> Give me a kiss, and to that kiss a score;
> Then to that twenty, add a hundred more:
> A thousand to that hundred: so kiss on,
> To make that thousand up a million.
> Treble that million, and when that is done,
> Let's kiss afresh, as when we first begun.

Acknowledgements

Grateful acknowledgement is made to the authors of the works listed in the bibliography and cited in the text.

It is with pleasure that I thank my publisher, Iris Tupholme, who first encouraged this history of kissing; I could not have written this book without her high standards and support.

Warm thanks to my editors, Siobhan Blessing and Nicole Langlois, for nurturing this book from conception to completion. Working with these talented individuals will remain one of the most luminous experiences in my life.

My thanks and gratitude to Allyson Latta for her superb copy editing, to Lesley Barry for her wonderful attention to detail at the proofreading stage, to my publicist, Lisa Zaritzky, for her infectious enthusiasm, and to Akka Janssen and for her unflagging energy and dedication.

ACKNOWLEDGEMENTS

I am also deeply indebted to Kevin Gray for his visual acumen and generosity.

Abiding thanks to Suzanne Boyd for her loyalty—literary and otherwise.

And, for his ability to create magical Venetian moments, Alberto Gioia was the soaring winged lion that presided over the writing of this book.

My love and gratitude to my family. My mother has been a mainstay of encouragement.

Special thanks to my friends and colleagues Lory Dalla Monta, Christopher Dewdney, Marc Garand, Laurie Hellens, Michael Holmes, Tu Ly, Giorgio Milani, Mark Talacko and Zorheh Vakilian, whose support and comments on the manuscript were invaluable.

My gratitude to all the staff at HarperCollins Canada, whose support has been so vital.

Thank you to the librarians at the Toronto Reference Library, where much of this book was written.

And to Kit, who has taught me so much, a loving kiss.

Bibliography

Ackerman, Diane. *A Natural History of Love.* New York: Random House, 1994.

———. *A Natural History of the Senses.* New York: Random House, 1990.

Allende, Isabel. *Aphrodite: A Memoir of the Senses.* New York: Harper Perennial, 1998.

Andreae, Simon. *Anatomy of Desire: The Science and Psychology of Sex, Love and Marriage.* London: Little, Brown, 1998.

Angeloglou, Maggie. *A History of Make-up.* New York: The Macmillan Company, 1970.

Apuleius, Lucius. *The Golden Ass*, trans. Robert Graves. London: Penguin, 1985.

Balsdon, J.P.V.D. *Roman Women: Their History & Habits.* London; Toronto: Bodley Head, 1974.

Barash, David P., and Judith Eve Lipton. *Making Sense of Sex: How Genes and Gender Influence our Relationships.* Washington, D.C.: Island Press, 1997.

Barthes, Roland. *Fragments d'un discours amoureux.* Paris: Editions du Seuil, 1977.

Basten, Fred E. *Max Factor's Hollywood: Glamour, Movies, Makeup.* Los Angeles: General Publishing Group, 1995.

Berger, John. *The Sense of Sight.* New York: Pantheon Books, 1980.

Bergmann, Martin S. *The Anatomy of Loving.* New York: Columbia University Press, 1987.

Beroul. *The Romance of Tristran*, trans. Norris J.Lacy. New York: Garland Publishing, Inc.,1989.

Blue, Adrianne. *On Kissing: From the Metaphysical to the Erotic.* London: Victor Gollancz, 1996.

Blum, Deborah. *Sex on the Brain: The Biological Differences Between Men and Women.* New York: Viking,1997.

Bremmer, Jan and Roodenburg, Herman, eds. *A Cultural History of Gesture.* Cambridge: Polity Press, 1991.

Brillat-Savarin, Anthelme. *The Physiology of Taste,* trans. M.F.K. Fisher. Washington, D.C.: Counterpoint, 1999.

Bulfinch, Thomas. *Myths of Greece and Rome.* London: Penguin, 1981.

Burton, Richard Francis, Sir. *The Perfumed Garden.* Rochester: Park Street Press. 1992.

Burton, Robert. *The Language of Smell.* London: Routledge & Kegan Paul, 1976.

Buss, David M. *The Dangerous Passion: Why Jealousy is Necessary as Love and Sex.* New York: Free Press, 2000.

Camphausen, Rufus C. *The Encyclopedia of Sacred Sexuality.* Rochester, Vermont: Inner Traditions International, 1999.

Chang, Jolan. *The Tao of Love and Sex.* New York: EP Dutton, 1992.

Classon, Constance, David Homes, Anthony Synnoth. *Aroma: The Cultural History of Smell.* London; New York: Routledge, 1994.

Colette. *Cheri and the Last of Cheri.* New York: Farrar Straus & Young, 1953.

Cooke, Deryck. *The Language of Music.* London: Oxford University Press, 1987.

Corson, Richard. *Fashions in Makeup: From Ancient to Modern Times.* London: Peter Owen Limited, 1972.

Crenshaw, Theresa L. *The Alchemy of Love and Lust.* New York: G.P. Putnam's Sons, 1996.

Dante. *The Divine Comedy of Dante Alighieri*, trans. Allen Mandelbaum. 3 vols. New York; Toronto; London; Sydney; Auckland: Bantam Books, 1982.

Darwin, Charles. *The Descent of Man, and Selection in Relation to Sex*. New York: Collier, 1963.

de Beauvoir, Simone. *Letters to Sartre*, trans./ed. Quintin Hoare. London: Random Century Group Ltd., 1991.

de Castelbajac, Kate. *The Face of the Century: 100 Years of Makeup and Style*. New York: Rizzoli, 1995.

de Maupassant, Guy. *The Complete Short Stories of Guy de Maupassant*, ed. Artine Artinian. Garden City, N.Y.: Doubleday & Company, Inc., 1955.

de Rouche, Max. *The Foods of Love*. Boston: Little, Brown, 1991.

de Waal, Frans, & Frans, Lanting. *Bonobo: The Forgotten Ape*. Berkeley and Los Angeles: University of California Press, 1977.

Dewdney, Christopher. *Last Flesh: Life in the Transhuman Era*. Toronto: HarperCollins Publishers Ltd., 1998.

———. *The Secular Grail*. Toronto: Somerville House Publishing, 1993.

Durrell, Lawrence. *Justine*. London: Faber and Faber, 1968.

Ellis, Havelock. *On Life and Sex: Essays of Love and Virtue*. Garden City: Garden City Publishing Company, 1937.

———. *Studies in the Psychology of Sex*. Vol. 1. New York: Random House, 1936.

Endleman, Robert. *Love and Sex in Twelve Cultures*. New York: Psyche Press, 1989.

Fisher, Helen. *Anatomy of Love: A Natural History of Mating, Marriage, and Why We Stray*. New York: W. W. Norton, 1992.

Fisher, Helen. *The Sex Contract: The Evolution of Human Behavior*. New York: William Morror and Company, Inc., 1982.

Foucault, Michel. *The History of Sexuality*, trans. R. Hurley. 3 vols. New York: Pantheon Books, 1990.

Fraser, Antonia ed. *Love Letters: An Anthology*. London: Weidenfeld and Nicolson, 1976.

Freud, Sigmund. *On Sexuality: Three Essays of the Theory of Sexuality*. Harmondsworth: Penguin, 1977.

Friedman, Mariam. *The Kiss.* New York: Universe Books, 1976.
Fromm, Erich. *The Art of Loving.* New York: Harper & Row, 1956.
Genders, Roy. *Perfume Through the Ages:* New York: Putnam, 1972.
Gilson, E. *Heloise and Abelard.* London: Hollis & Carter, 1953.
Goodall, Jane. *The Chimpanzees of Gombe: Patterns in Behavior.* Cambridge, Mass.: Belknap Press, 1986.
Gould, James L., Gould, Carol Grant. *Sexual Selection: Mate Choice and Courtship in Nature.* New York: Scientific American Library, 1989.
Grandidier, Alfred. *Souvenir de Voyages (1865–1870).* Antananarivo: Association malgache d'Archéologie, 1971.
Groom, Nigel. *Perfume: The Ultimate Guide to the World's Finest Fragrances.* Philadelphia: Running Press, 1999.
Grunfeld, Frederic. *Rodin.* New York: Holt, Fitzhenry & Whiteside, 1987.
Haedrich, Marcel. *Coco Chanel: Her Life Her Secrets.* Toronto: Little Brown & Company, 1972.
Harris, Nathaniel. *History of Ancient Rome.* London: Hamlyn, 2000.
Heylbut, Rose. *Like Softest Music: Love Stories of Famous Composers.* New York: Thomas Y. Crowell Company, 1936.
Hobson, Polly. *Venus and her Prey.* London: Constable, 1975.
James, Henry. *The Portrait of a Lady.* Oxford: Oxford University Press, 1998.
Jankowiak, William. *Romantic Passion: A Universal Experience.* New York: Columbia University Press, 1995.
Johns, Catherine. *Sex or Symbol: Erotic Images of Greece and Rome.* London: Colonnade Books: British Museum Publications Limited, 1982.
Kelly, Walter Keating. *Erotica: The Elegies of Propertius, The Satyricon of Petronius Arbi and The Kisses of Johannes Secundus. . . .* London: Bohn, 1854.
Kern, Stephen. *The Culture of Love: Victorians to Moderns.* Cambridge: Harvard University Press, 1992.
Kerzweil, Ray. *The Age of Spiritual Machines.* New York: Viking, 1999.
Khatchadourian, Herant. *Biological Aspects of Human Sexuality.* New York: Holt, Rinehart & Winston, 1987.

Kiefer, Otto. *Sexual Life in Ancient Rome*. London: Constable and Company Limited, 1994.

Kohl, James Vaughn and Robert T. Francoeur. *The Scent of Eros: Mysteries of Odor in Human Sexuality*. New York: Continuum, 1995.

Labé, Louise. *Elegies et Sonnets*. Paris: Baudouin, n.d.

Lake, Max. *Scents and Sensuality: The Essence of Excitement*. London: J. Murray, 1989.

LeVay Simon. *The Sexual Brain*. Cambridge, Mass.: MIT Press, 1993.

Liebowitz, Michael. *The Chemistry of Love*. Boston: Little, Brown, 1983.

Lloyd, Rosemary. *Closer and Closer Apart: Jealousy in Literature*. New York: Cornell University Press, 1995.

Lucie-Smith, Edward. *Ars Erotica: An Arousing History of Erotic Art*. New York: Rizzoli, 1997.

Lucie-Smith, Edward. *Sexuality in Western Art*. New York: Thames and Hudson, 1972.

MacLean, Paul. *A Triune Concept of the Brain and Behavior*. Toronto: University of Toronto Press, 1973.

Malinowsky, Bronislaw. *The Sexual Life of Savages*. London: Routledge, 1932.

Marin, Rick. *Hug-Hug, Kiss-Kiss: It's a Jungle Out There*. The New York Times, September 19, 1999.

Masson, Georgina. *Courtesans of the Italian Renaissance*. London: Secker & Warburg, 1975.

Masters, John. *Casanova*. New York: Bernard Geis Associates, 1969.

Masters, William H. and Virginia Johnson. *Human Sexual Response*. Boston: Little, Brown, 1966.

McNeill, Daniel. *The Face*. Boston: Little, Brown, 1998.

Menkes, Vivienne (trans.). *Three Seconds from Eternity: Photographs by Robert Doisneau*. Boston: New York Graphic Society, 1979.

Mills, Jane. *Bloomsbury Guide to Erotic Literature*. London: Bloomsbury, 1993.

Money, John. *Love & Love Sickness: The Science of Sex, Gender Difference, and Pair Bonding*. Baltimore: John Hopkins University Press, 1980.

Montagu, Ashley. *Touching: The Human Significance of the Skin*. New York: Colombia University Press, 1971.

Montreynaud, Florence. *Love: A Century of Love and Passion*. Paris, Edition du Chene-Hachette Livre, 1997.

Morris, Edwin T. *Fragrance: The Story of Perfume from Cleopatra to Chanel*. New York: Scribner's, 1986.

Morris, Desmond. *Babywatching*. New York: Crown Publishers, Inc., 1992.

Morris, Desmond. *The Naked Ape Trilogy*. London: J. Cape, 1994.

Morton, Marcia and Frederick. *Chocolate: An Illustrated History*. New York: Crown Publishers, 1986.

Newman, Cathy. *Perfume: The Art and Science of Scent*. Washington, D.C.: National Geographic Society, 1998.

Newman, Jenny, ed. *The Faber Book of Seductions*. London; Boston: Faber and Faber Limited, 1988.

Newton, Helmut. *Pola Woman*. Munich: Schirmer / Mosel, 1992.

Nin, Anaïs. *The Diary of Anaïs Nin*. Vol 1. New York: Swallow Press, 1966; New Haven, Conn.: Yale University Press, 1988.

———. *Little Birds: Erotica by Anaïs Nin*. New York: Harcourt Brace Jovanovich, 1979.

Nyrop, Christopher. *The Kiss and Its History*, trans. W.F. Harvey. London: Sands, 1901.

Orczy, Baroness. *The Scarlett Pimpernel*. London: Hodder & Stoughton, 1961.

Ovid [Pioblus Ovidius Naso]. *The Art of Love*. New York: Grosset & Dunlap, Inc., 1954.

———. *Metamorphoses*, trans. R. Humphries. Bloomingdale, Ind.: Indiana University Press, 1955.

Paz, Octavio. *The Double Flame: Love and Eroticism*. San Diego, New York, London: Harcourt Brace & Company, 1993.

Perella, Nicolas James. *The Kiss: Sacred and Profane*. Berkeley and Los Angeles: University of California Press, 1969.

Phillips, Adam. *On Kissing, Tickling, and Being Bored*. London: Faber and Faber, 1993.

Pope, A. *'Eloisa to Abelard', Collected Poems*, ed. Bonamy Dobrée. London; New York: J.M. Dent & Sons, 1976.

Pound, Ezra. *The Translations of Ezra Pound*. New York: New Directions, 1953.

Proust, Marcel. *Remembrance of Things Past*, trans. C.K. Scott

Moncrieff and Frederick A. Blossom. 2 vols. New York: Random House, Inc., 1932.

Pullar, Philippa. *Consuming Passions: A History of English Food and Appetite*. London: H. Hamilton, 1970.

Ragas, Meg Cohen, Karen Kozlowski. *Read My Lips: A Cultural History of Lipstick*. San Francisco: Chronicle Books, 1998.

Reed, Myrtle. *Love Affairs of Literary Men*. New York, London: G.P. Putnam's Sons, The Knickerbocker Press, 1907.

Reichold, Klaus and Bernhard Graf. *Paintings that Changed the World: From Lascaux to Picasso*. Munich, London, New York: Prestel, 1998.

Reinisch, June M.; Beasley, Ruth. *The Kinsey Institute New Report on Sex: What You Must Know to be Sexually Literate*. New York: St. Martin's Press, 1990.

Riefenstahl, Leni. *People of Kau*. London: Wm. Collins Sons & Co. Ltd., 1976.

Roth, Geneen. *Feeding the Hungry Heart: The Experience of Compulsive Eating*. New York: Signet, 1982.

Savage-Rumbaugh, Sue; Stuart G. Shanker, and Talbot J. Taylor. *Apes, Language, and the Human Mind*. New York: Oxford University Press, Inc., 1998.

Schulze, Franz. *Philip Johnson: Life and Work*. New York: Alfred A. Knopf, 1994.

Shakespeare, William. *Romeo and Juliet*, ed. T.J.B. Spencer. New York: Penguin, 1967.

Shakespeare, William. *Venus and Adonis*, ed. Humphrey Jennings. London: Alces Press, 1993.

Shipman, David. *Caught in the Act: Sex and Eroticism in the Movies*. London: Elm Tree Books, 1985.

Smith, David B., Robert F. Margolskee. *Making Sense of Taste*. Scientific American, March 2001.

Stendhal (Marie Henri Beyle). *Love*, trans. Gilbert and Suzanne Sale. New York: Penguin, 1975.

Stoker, Bram. *Bram Stoker's Dracula Omnibus*. London: Virgin, 1992.

Tannahill, Reay. *Sex in History*. New York: Stein and Day / Scarborough House, 1992.

Theimer, Ernst Theo. *Fragrance Chemistry: The Science of the Sense of Smell*. New York; Toronto: Academic Press, 1982.

Thomas, Lewis. *The Lives of a Cell: Notes of a Biology Watcher*. New York: Penguin Putnam Inc., 1978.

Thompson Lowell, Carrie. *The True Lovers' Treasury: Famous Lovers in Literature*. Boston: Colonial Press, 1907.

Trueman, John. *The Romantic Story of Scent* . Garden City, N.Y.: Doubleday, 1975.

Velde, Theodoor H. van de. *Ideal Marriage: Its Physiology and Technique*. London: Heinemann, 1962.

Vroon, Piet. *Smell: The Secret Seducer*. New York: Farrar, Straus and Giroux, 1997.

Wagner, Peter. *Eros Revived: Erotica of the Enlightenment in England and America*. London: Secker and Warburg, 1988.

Walters, Mark Jerome. *The Dance of Life: Courtship in the Animal Kingdom*. New York: Arbor House, 1988.

Walton, Alan Hull. *Aphrodisiacs: From Legend to Prescription*. Westport, Conn.: Associated Booksellers, 1958.

Washington, Peter (ed.). *Love Letters*. London: David Campbell Publishers Ltd., 1996.

Watson, Lyall. *Jacobson's Organ and the Remarkable Nature of Smell*. New York; London: W.W. Norton & Company, 2000.

Wedeck, Harry Ezekiel. *Dictionary of Aphrodisiacs*. New York: Philosophical Library, 1961.

Westheimer, Ruth. *The Art of Arousal: A Celebration of Erotic Art Throughout History*. Lanham; New York; Oxford: Madison Books, 1993.

Index

Page citations in *italic* below refer to *marginalia*.

Abelard & Heloise, 161–62
Abom, Shana, 42
A Fool There Was (film), 172
Aimée & Jaguar (film), 188
air kisses. *See* kisses, air
alchemy, 5, *11*, 28, *108*, *193*
"A l'heure de observatoire—les amoureux" by Man Ray, *147*, 147–48
"Allegory with the Triumph of Venus" by Bronzino, 134–36, *135*
Allegri, Antonio. *See* Correggio
androstenone, 92–93
Angeloglou, Maggie, 193
anticipation, its role in seduction, *123*
Antony, Mark (Roman General), 90, 122–23
aphrodisiacs, 100
A Place in the Sun (film), 176
Apuleius, Lucius (c. 123–c. 170), 18
Ariosto, Ludovico (1474–1533), 101
A Room with a View (film), 182
"As above, so below" (dictum), *61*
Ashby, Hal, 178
Aspasia (c. 470–410 B.C.), 122
Astor, Mary, *172*
Auden, W.H., 108
Augustine. *See* Saint Augustine

Bacall, Lauren, 175
baiser, mistranslations of, *46*

Ball, Lucille, 199, 201
Banderas, Antonio, 196
Bara, Theda (1890–1955), 171–72
Baroque (painting movement), *136*
Barrymore, John (1882–1942), *172*
Baudelaire, Charles, 83, 91
Beauhamais, Joséphine. *See* Napoleon Bonaparte & Joséphine
Beauty and the Beast, story of, 158
Bécquer, Gustavo Adolfo, 205
Behn, Aphra, 164–65
Bergman, Ingrid, 175
Binoche, Juliette, 185
Blake, William (1757–1827), *71*
Blanchett, Cate, 200
the Blarney Stone, 12
body language. *See* synchrony, interactional
Bogart, Humphrey, 175
Bonaparte, Napoleon. *See* Napoleon Bonaparte & Joséphine
Bonham-Carter, Helena, 182
bonobos, 112–14
Boucher, François (1703–1770), 138–39, 142
Bow, Clara, 206
Brawne, Fanny, *208*
breasts, 7, 28, 80, 82, 84, 105
  sensuousness of, 28–29, *105*, *135*, *139*
Breton, Nicholas (1542–1626), 170
Bridges, Robert (1844–1930), 27

INDEX

Brillat-Savarin, Jean-Anthelme, 100
Brochet, Anne, 180
Brontë, Charlotte (1816–1865), 158
Bronzino, Agnolo (1503–1572), 134–36
Brosnan, Pierce, 187
Browning, Elizabeth Barrett (1806–1861), 162–63
Browning, Robert (1812–1889), 75, 90, 110, 142, 163
Buck, Detlev, 189
Burns, Robert (1759–1796), 69
Burton, Sir Richard, 61
Byron, Lord (1788–1824), 53, 67

camera obscura (photographic technique), *150*
Campbell, Thomas (1777–1844), 13
Canova, Antonio (1757–1822), 139–40
Casanova, Giovanni Giacomo (1725–1798), *106*, 124
Catullus (87–c. 54 B.C.), 36
Cervantes, Miguel de (1547–1616), 66
Champagne (beverage), *44*
Chanel, Coco (Gabrielle), 94
Ch'en Meng-Chia, 40
chimney sweeps, 59–60
chocolate, 104–6
  derivation of, *105*
Cinema Paradiso (film), 179
Clef de Coquette, 203
Cleopatra (69–30 B.C.), 89–90, 96, 122–23, 194
Clift, Montgomery, 176–77
clitoris, sensuousness of, 34
Colette (the novelist), 45
colour. *See also* red (the colour)
  sensuousness of, 62, 146, 194–95, 200–209
  shifting look of, 196
Congreve, William (1610–1729), 12
Conrad, Joseph, 17
copulation, ancient art portraying, 128
Correggio (c. 1489–1534), 132–34

"Cupid and Psyche" by Canova, 139–40, *139–40*
Cupid and Psyche, the myth of, 139–41
Cyrano de Bergerac (film), 180

Dali, Salvador, 163
dancing, sensuousness of, 79
Dante Alighieri (1265–1321), 155, 164
da Vinci, Leonardo, 72
Davis, Bette, 198, 201
Day-Lewis, Daniel, 183
de Beaumont, Marie Le Prince, 158
de Beauvior, Simone (1908–1986), 168–69
Dekker, Thomas (1572–1632), *68*
de Medici, Catherine, 96
de Musset, Alfred (1810–1857), 5
Depardieu, Gérard, 180
desire, 19, 27–28, 56–57, 81, 88, 107–8, 110, 121, 152–53, 166, 192, 200, *201*
de Villeneuve, Gabrielle, 158
de Waal, Frans, 113–14
Dewdney, Christopher, 76–77
Diaz, Cameron, 71
Dietrich, Marlene, 123, 188
disease, kissing and fears of, 51
divorce, 110
Doisneau, Robert (1912–1944), 151
Don Juan (film), 172
Donne, John (1572–1631), 26
d'Orchamps, Baroness, 195
Douglas, Lord Alfred, 17
Dreiser, Theodore, 176
Drouet, Juliette, 166
Druids, 13
Drummond, William (of Hawthornden; 1585–1649), 80, 178
Dunaway, Faye, 187
Dunst, Kirsten, 13
Duplessis, Marie (1824–1847), 123
Durrell, Lawrence, 68, 160

Eliot, George (1819–1880), 26, 99

223

INDEX

Elliott, Denholm, 182
Ellis, Havelock (1859–1939), 119
Eluard, Paul, 163
endorphins, 60, 78, 80, 87
The English Patient (film), 185
Ennius (c. 239–c.169 B.C.), 36
eyes, erogenous expression with the, 66–69

Factor, Max, 197–98
Färberböck, Max, 188
the fashion trade, kissing and, 50–52
fellatio. *See also* kisses, genital, 61, 64
Fiennes, Ralph, 185
film noir, defined, *189*
films. *See* kisses, cinematic; *See also specific exemplars, e.g.* Gone with the Wind
Firenzuola (Italian monk), 194
Fisher, Helen E., 121
Flaubert, Gustave, 129, *139*
Florence (Italian city), *182*, 182–83
Forster, E.M. (1897–1970), 182, *183*
Fragonard, Jean-Honoré (1732–1806), 142
Francesca & Paolo, Dante's story of, 155–56
Freud, Sigmund, 6–7, 144
From Here to Eternity (film), 177
Fuller, Margaret Witter (1810–1850), 132

Gable, Clark, 173
Gainsborough, Thomas, 201
Garbo, Greta, 123, 206
Gardner, Ava, 206
Garland, Judy, 198
Gay, John (1685–1732), 174, 182
Gere, Richard, 184
Gibson, Dr. Henry (1808–1884), 73
Giotto (1267–1337), 129–30
gloves, scented, 96
gods of love, 36
Gone with the Wind (film), 173

Gordon, Ruth, 178
Gorges, Arthur (1557–1625), 77
Grant, Cary, 175
Graves, Rupert, 183
Grillparzer, Franz (1791–1872), 48
Gutenberg, Johann (c. 1397–1466), *154*

Hafiz, "Diwan" (1320–1391), *201*
hair, facial, *81*, 81–82
"halo effect." *See* "love maps"
hands
  kissing of, 24, 26, 31, 48, *49*
  smelling of, 21–22
handshakes, 25, 49–50
Harlow, Jean, 198
Harold and Maude (film), 178
Hays, William H., 172
Hays Code (governing film kisses, etc.), 172–73
Hayworth, Rita, 198
hearing, sensuousness of, 75–79, *76*
Hebbel, Friedrich, 165
Heine, Heinrich (1797–1856), 15, 19
Heinsius, Daniel (1580–1655), 120
Herbert, Edward (Lord Cherbury; 1583–1648), 107, 144
"*Hercules and Omphale*" by Boucher, 138–39
Herman-Wurmfeld, Charles, 190
Hermaphroditus, 15
Herrick, Robert (1591–1674), 3, 66, 164, 211
Higgins, Colin, 178
Hilda and Rango, story of, 160–61
Hitchcock, Alfred, 175–76, 187
Holmes, Oliver Wendell (1809–1894), 75
Holty, Ludwig Christoph Heinrich (1748–1776), *18*
Hugo, Victor (1802–1885), 54, 166
Hunt, Leigh (1784–1859), 18

index, puzzling self-reference to, 224
infatuation. *See* lovesickness

INDEX

Ingram, Rex, 198
instincts, kissing and, 6–7

James, Henry, 9
Jane Eyre, story of, 158–60
jealousy, 118–20, *119*
Jolie, Angelina, 206
Jones, James, 177
Jonson, Ben (1573–1637), 67, 74
Judas (the traitor), kisses of, 17
Juergensen, Heather, 190
Jung, Carl Gustav, *108*
"Jupiter and Io" by Correggio, *133*, 133–34

Kalidasa (fifth century poet), 97
Kama Sutra of Vatsayana, 28–31, *31*, 34
Keats, John (1795–1821), 82, *208*
Kerr, Deborah, 177
King Henry II (France), 96
Kipling, Rudyard, 177
The Kiss, May Irwin–John C. Rice (film), 171
"The Kiss" by Klimt, 144, *145*
"The Kiss" by Rodin, 130–32, *131*
kisses. *See also* kissing; lips; weddings
　air, 50–51
　of betrayal, 17–18
　cinematic, 170–91
　cool water and, *45*
　cultural differences and, 21–24, 27
　of death, *100*, 129
　evaluations of, 56
　eyelash (aka butterfly), 69
　farewell (the final), *26*, 26–27
　first, x, 53–57
　French, 43–47
　genital, 60–65
　in June, *58*
　Kama Sutra, 29–31
　matrimonial, 57–60
　memories of, 210–11
　ruinous, 119

sniff, 40–43
social status and, 22
songs about, 79
sound and, 75–79
stolen, 18–19, *121*, 142
telephone, 76
unwanted, 53
kissing. *See also* disease; hands; instincts; kisses
　animals and, *115*, 129
　calories required while, 199
　ceremonial, 53
　corporate. *See* kissing, social expectations and variations in
　desire and. *See also* desire, 19
　erotic lovemaking and, 8, 20, 23–24, 27–29, 80–81
　as an exchange or merging of souls, 4, 15, 23, 25, *25*, 40–43, 58, 153, 164–65
　of the ground and feet, 10, 14, 19, 24–26, 84
　head-turn directional preferences and, *5*
　as a healing act, 11
　love and, 9, 15–16
　Max Factor's test machine for, 199
　meanings of, 3, 8, 21–23, 35
　motivations for & origins of, 4–7, 10
　powers assumed to be gained by, 10–12, 14
　reputed benefits of, 60, *60*
　to seal a signature mark, 25
　signifying or creating peace, 25–26
　social expectations and variations in, 51–53
　synonyms for, *4*
　as taboo in public, 23, 32, 35, 46
　teeth and, 102
　as veneration, 21, 26
Kissing Jessica Stein (film), 190
Klimt, Gustav (1862–1918), 144
Köhler, Juliane, 189
Kurzweil, Ray, *112*

INDEX

Labé, Louise, 20
Lancaster, Burt, 177
Lancelot & Guinevere, the passions of, 156
Lanting, Frans, 113
"Leda and the Swan"
  (anon. at Herculaneum), 129
  by Reubens, 136–38, *137*
Leigh, Vivien, 173
letters, of love, 166–69, *166*, *168–69*
Lichtenstein, Roy (1923–1997), 148–49
lips. *See also* mouths
  collagen implants in, 207
  fashions in, 206
  French kisses and, 47
  moistening of, 73
  ornamentation of, 22
  sensuousness of, x, 28–29, 34, 62, 73–74, 205–9
  as signposts, 200
  squeezing of, 29
  synonyms for the, 28, 32
  vocabularies invoking, 74
lipsticks, x, 62, 192–204
  history of, 202–3
  sensuousness of, 202–4
love, biochemistry and, 107–8
love letters. *See* letters, of love
"love maps," 110–11
lovers
  fictional, *161*
  various famous, 154–63, *164*
lovesickness, 108–10
Lucretius (99–55 B.C.), 43
Ly, Tu, 207–9

Madonna, 123, 201
Magritte, René, 148
Maguire, Tobey, 13
Malinowski, Bronislaw, 23
Man Ray (1890–1976), 146–47, 199
Mare Nostrum (film), 198
Marlowe, Christopher (1564–1593), 10, 67, 104

marriage, three types of, 59
massage, 85
Mata Hari (1876–1917), 123
Max Factor Museum (Hollywood), 197–98
McQueen, Steve, 187
McTieman, John, 187
Michelangelo, 136
Miller, Henry, 160–61
Minghella, Anthony, 185
"mirroring." *See* synchrony, interactional
mistletoe, 13–14
Mitchell, Margaret, 173
Monroe, Marilyn, 123, 201, 206
Moore, Thomas (1779–1852), 73
Morocco (film), 188
Morris, Desmond, 6, 11
Morsztyn, Jan Andrzej, 200
mouths. *See also* lips; tongues
  bacterial flora of, 102
  hygiene and, 16
  physiology of, 6
Mozart, Wolfgang Amadeus (1756–1791), 166
music, sensuousness of, 78–79
musk, 92
Muzio, Girolamo, 164

Napoleon Bonaparte & Joséphine, 94, 167–68
Nefertiti (Egyptian Queen), 194
Nefwazi, Sheik Shaykh, 61, 75–76, 102–3
Newton, Helmut, 150–51
Nikarchos (Greek poet), 52
Nin, Anaïs, 160–61
nipples, 6, 34, 85, 87
noses, kissing and. *See* kisses, sniff
Notorious (film), 175, 187

O'Keeffe, Georgia (1887–1986), 200
Ondaatje, Michael, 185
Orsini, Flavio (Prince of Nerola), 95–96

INDEX

Ovid (43 B.C.–c. 18 A.D.), 35, 37–40, 70, 152, 192
oxytocin (hormone), 80, 84–85

Pascal, Blaise, 179
Patmore, Coventry (1823–1896), 118
penis. *See also* phalli
    synonyms for the, 32, 61
Perez, Vincent, 180
perfumes, 94–96
Pericles (of Athens), 122
phalli, 127–28
    as good luck charms, 128
pheromones. *See also* perfumes, 90–94, 92
Picasso, Pablo (1881–1973), 145–46
Picasso, Paloma, 150, 200
Plato, 164
Pop Art (painting movement), *148*
Pound, Ezra, 121
pre-mastication (of food offerings), 5, 43
Pretty Woman (film), 184, 206
Propertius, Sextus (c. 54 B.C.–c. 2 A.D.), 35, 66, 149
Proust, Marcel, 16
psychoneuroimmunology (PNI), 111
Pygmalion (Ovid's version), 39–40

Queen Elizabeth I, 12

Rappeneau, Jean-Paul, 180
red (the colour), 200, 200–202
Renaissance art, *129*
Reubens, Peter Paul (1577–1640), 136–37
Rilke, Rainer Maria (1875–1926), 132, 165
Roberts, Julia, 184, 206
Rococo (painting movement), *138*
Rodin, Auguste (1840–1917), 130–31
Rogers, Ginger, 198
Romeo & Juliet, love story of, 156–58
roses. *See also* perfumes, 89–90, 91

Rossetti, Christina, 60
Rossetti, Dante Gabriel (1830–1894), 89, 165
Rostand, Edmond (1868–1918), *180*, 180–81
Roth, Geneen, 105
RuPaul, 207
Russo, Rene, 187

Saint Augustine, 25
saliva, 22–24, 28, 32, 101–4
Sands, Julian, 183
Sappho, 36–37, 89, 109
Sartre, Jean-Paul (1908–1980), 168–69
Saxe, J.G. (1816–1887), 165
The Scarlet Pimpernel, 19
Schiffer, Claudia, 207–9
Schrader, Maria, 189
the Seal of Solomon, *58*
Secundus, Johannes, 8, 165
seduction, 120–24, *123*–24
The Seven Year Itch (film), 206
sexual activity, types of, *110*
Shakespeare, William (1564–1616), 21, 24, 57, 69, 78, 87, 100, 152–53, 156, 197, 202
Shelley, Percy Bysshe (1792–1822), 98, 164
shoplifting, lipstick and, 193
sights, arousing nature of, 67–69, 149–51
Silentiarius, Paulus (?–c. 575), 127
skin, sensuousness of, 82–86
Sleeping Beauty, 18–19
smelling
    physiology of, 88
    as precursor to sniff-kisses, 42–43
smells
    the importance of, *43*
    sensuousness of, 86–97
smiling, 70–72
Smith, Maggie, 182
Stendhal, *182*
Stevens, George, 176

INDEX

Stoker, Bram, 17
suckling, 6–7
Surrealism (painting movement), *146*
Swinburne, Algemon C. (1837–1909), *78*, *116*
synchrony, interactional, 115–17
Syrus, Publilius, 77

Tantrism, 32–34
Taoist tradition, *28*
taste. *See also* tongues
  metaphors making use of, 99, *101*
  physiology of, 97–98, *99*
  sensuousness of, 97–101
Taylor, Elizabeth, 176
Taylor, Estelle, *172*
temperature (body), kissing and, 8
Tennyson, Alfred Lord (1809–1892), 5, *101*, 154, 206
Tertullian (c. 160–c. 240), 58
testosterone, 92
Thomas, Kristin Scott, 185
Thomas, Lewis, 92
The Thomas Crown Affair (film), *187*
Thompson, James Maurice (1844–1901), 90
To Have and Have Not (film), *175*
Tolstoy, Leo, 169
tongues, 204
  caressing the neck or ears, 47
  French kisses and, 6–8, 23, 30, 34, 43–47
  sensitivity of, 8–9, *84*
  vocabularies invoking, 74
Tornatore, Giuseppe, 179

Toskan, Frank, 207
touch
  metaphors making use of, 85–86
  sensuousness of, 80–86, *84*
Tristan *&* Isolde, legend of, 154–55
Tunghsuan (Chinese Master), 31–32

vaginas, 33–34, 60–61
vampires, kisses of, 17, 206
van de Velde, Theodore Hendrik, 44
Vidyapati (poet), 55–56
Vikings, 48–49
vocalization, kisses and, 33
voices (human), expressiveness of, 77
von Schiller, Johann Christoph Friedrich, 27
vulva, synonyms for the, 32, 61

Warhol, Andy, *148*
Water of Life, *102*
weddings, kisses at, 59
West, Mae, 123–24, *173*
Westfeldt, Jennifer, 190
Westheimer, Dr. Ruth, 134
Wilde, Oscar, 17, 119
Williams, Ester, 198
Wilmot, John (Earl of Rochester; 1637–1680), 114
Wolf, Toni, *108*
Wong, Anna May, *173*
Wu Hsien (Tao of Loving master), *28*

Zelle, Gertrud Margarete. *See* Mata Hari, 123
Zinnemann, Fred, 177